In this series we present people whose life stories, we believe, deserve a wide audience. Here are men and women who lived their lives for others. Here are people for whom the common good was paramount and for whom self-giving was, or became, the most natural thing in the world.

The individuals whose stories make up this series certainly had their faults and failings, but they're nonetheless people worthy of attention and emulation. They are flesh and blood heroes whose faith in God and concern for others make them role models for everyone.

OUT OF THE ORDINARY
NOVALIS Biographies

Gem: The Life of Sister Mac
Geraldine MacNamara

A Faith that Challenges
The Life of Jim McSheffrey

Fateful Passages
The Life of Henry Somerville,
Catholic Journalist

Fateful Passages

Fateful Passages

The Life of Henry Somerville, Catholic Journalist

Joseph Sinasac

NOVALIS

© 2003 Novalis, Saint Paul University, Ottawa, Canada

Cover: Blair Turner
Layout: Richard Proulx

Business Office:
Novalis
49 Front Street East, 2nd Floor
Toronto, Ontario, Canada
M5E 1B3

Phone: 1-877-702-7773 or (416) 363-3303
Fax: 1-877-702-7775 or (416) 363-9409
E-mail: cservice@novalis.ca
www.novalis.ca

National Library of Canada Cataloguing in Publication

Sinasac, Joseph P. (Joseph Patrick), 1957–
    Fateful passages : the life of Henry Somerville, Catholic
journalist / Joseph Sinasac.

    ISBN 2-89507-403-8

1. Somerville, Henry, 1889-1953. 2. Journalists–Canada–Biography.
3. Press, Catholic–Canada–History–20th century. I. Title.

PN4874.S598S55 2003   070.92   C2003-904091-7

We acknowledge the financial support of the Government of Canada through
the Book Publishing Industry Development Program (BPIDP) for our
publishing activities.

5 4 3 2 1   07 06 05 04 03

This book is dedicated to Eleanor Warren,
my aunt and godmother,
who awakened the writer inside me.

Contents

Acknowledgments

An author's strongest moment of gratitude comes when the completed manuscript sits in a pile of neat white pages on the desk before him. With a sigh of relief, he can look back with fondness on all those who helped bring this seemingly never-ending task to a successful end (successful being defined as *done*). Now is that time for me.

First mention must go to the surviving children of Henry Somerville – Stephen, Moira and Janet – whose enthusiastic encouragement and co-operation ensured that their father could be depicted as a fully rounded human being, and not just a figure behind a typewriter. Their vivid recollections of family life and their willingness to help me find important documents and photos have been invaluable.

Neither would this book have been possible without the groundwork of historian Jeanne Beck. Her doctoral thesis on our subject's thought and work gave me a framework around which to build this biography, and a long list of necessary facts and leads. I do not even try in this short work to duplicate the scholarly quality of Beck's thesis – this is not an academic book in any case – but I can attest that her work and friendly advice made my job much easier.

Help came from many other quarters. Dr. Mark McGowan, a noted historian and principal of the University of St. Michael's College, provided numerous helpful leads. Marc Lerman, archivist for the Archdiocese of Toronto, took a personal interest in the project and made my work that much easier. Monsignor Tom Raby and Alfred de Manche gave me useful personal insights into the workings of *The Catholic Register* during Somerville's later years, as did Father Joe O'Neill. Peter McGuigan filled in the blanks on a vitally important episode in the history of *The Register* in 1948 when it was temporarily supplanted by *The Ensign*, and kindly allowed me to use an academic article he has written on the subject.

All their work has found a place, one way or another, in this book. All interpretations of the facts – and any mistakes – are of course mine alone.

Lastly, I must thank my wife, Tawny, and children, David and Sarah, for putting up with my pre-occupation with this task over these last two years. Not to mention my hogging the computer.

Joseph Sinasac
Toronto, Canada
March 31, 2003

Foreword

My first memory is of a dingy corridor in the Ford Hotel, which stood at the corner of Dundas and Bay Streets in Toronto, Canada, long ago. This was the new country and city to which Henry Somerville, my father, had led his family from England in September 1933, when I was two-and-a-half years old, my brother, Peter, four, and my sister, Anne, six weeks. (Moira and Janet, the "Canucks" in our family, were born later.) All I can remember is that dark hotel corridor and the sweet fruit candies with colourful wrappers that Dad wisely caused to appear at that stressful moment of arriving in a strange land.

Later on, I remember candies coming home with Dad regularly after work on Fridays, in modest amounts, and never on other days, unless they were festive ones. Mum and Dad were never guilty of spoiling us with creature comforts. But Sundays, feast days, birthdays and the like were days of special delight, never lavish but always genuine. And rather serious.

As we five children grew up and developed our own minds, talents and personalities, it gradually became clear that our father and mother, in quite contrasting ways, were greatly gifted persons and parents. Dad had a formidable intellect, was largely self-educated with a prodigious capacity for reading and remembering. He acquired a vast competence in serious journalism and Catholic social teaching, not to mention the humanities, theology and other related fields. This is not the place to parade the qualities of Margaret, our incomparable mother, his wisely chosen wife. But let me note that I never once heard them quarrel, nor saw any one of us five punished physically. Dad could threaten, but rarely did, and his immense natural authority prevailed. Yes, we had a certain fear of him, but I think it was more formative than harmful, and I am sure it was later cast out by love.

Dad's faith in God and in the Catholic Church was powerful and all-embracing. I leave this book to help illuminate that faith. But after his death, I saw it shine out in his written marriage proposal to my future mother, and a corresponding radiance in her reply. (She had committed both letters to my care.) They led us children in faithful daily prayer year after year. They never wilfully missed Sunday Mass.

Dad died (rather beautifully and consciously, and all seven of us were together at the end) in early 1953. He predeceased the great preconciliar Pope Pius XII by a good five years, and the Second Vatican Council by another four. He was only 63 years old. Had he lived longer, would he have joined the revolutionary 1960s, or relaxed his religious faith as so many millions have since done? I cannot imagine it.

I remember the great void that I felt in my life when his ready learning and wisdom and "Catholic habit" were no longer available to me, just when I was starting to appreciate his rich resources more fully and maturely. How grateful I am to those who conceived and planned and brought about this book. How confirmed in sonship by my two surviving siblings (those two "Canuck" sisters, and the best of my friends), who deferred to me the honour of writing this Foreword.

I hope and pray that you will gather a blessing, through this book, from God, "from whom every fatherhood in heaven and on earth is named" (Ephesians 3:15).

Father Stephen Somerville
May 15, 2003

A Working-class Boy

And did the Countenance Divine
Shine forth upon our clouded hills?
And was Jerusalem builded here,
Among these dark Satanic Mills?

William Blake ("And Did Those Feet")

It was at the turn of the nineteenth century when William Blake recalled in verse the British myth that Jesus of Nazareth had once walked upon English sod, accompanied by Joseph of Arimathea. Blake was looking out on a British landscape being transformed by that symbol of the Industrial Revolution: the factory and its ubiquitous smokestack. Those belching, foul – "dark Satanic" – mills became an icon, for the poet, of a mechanistic, utilitarian world view he saw overwhelming Great Britain.

If he had lived to 1889 (he died in 1827), Blake would have found the full triumph of the mills in the English city of Leeds. Here in this West Yorkshire city the skyline was dominated not by the spires of churches, the usual landmarks of English provincial life, but by clouds of black smoke issuing from the narrow stacks rising above the peaked roofs of the factories. For, if nothing else, Leeds was at the heart of working, sweating industrial England. It was the home of the original sweatshop, marked by deep poverty, child labour and rampant disease, a city that Charles Dickens called in 1847 "the beastliest place, one of the nastiest I know." Understandably, it had been a hotbed of union activism for more than a century. In October of that year, 1889, it also was the birth-place of Henry Somerville.

Somerville was to become, if not a household name, a highly influential figure in Canadian Catholic Church circles in the mid-twentieth century. In a life as a journalist, social activist and defender of the Catholic faith, he would become one of the country's pre-eminent promoters of Catholic social teachings and a friend to the working class. Through columns, books, articles, lectures and even in the classroom, he worked tirelessly to help Catholic labourers understand modern economics and politics. In patient, jargon-free explanations he taught the often uneducated Catholic immigrants to Canada to use their faith as a prism through which to see current events and act to defend their own rights and those of the oppressed. His life's work would help to shape a social conscience among Catholics in Canada in much the same way that the better known Protestant "Social Gospellers" J.S. Woodsworth and Tommy Douglas would stir factory workers and farmers to create a left-wing political movement to complement the growing union movement of the time.

Though a resident of Canada for almost half his life, Henry Somerville was indelibly marked by Leeds, in all its coal-dust-coated glory. For the Leeds of Somerville's boyhood shaped the man and the beliefs that informed his actions for the rest of his life. To understand Somerville the man, then, it is necessary to know a little of life in Leeds at the turn of the twentieth century, as the Victorian era gave way to the Edwardian.

From early on in the Industrial Revolution, Leeds was its poster child, the sorry lesson municipal planners and political reformers held up as proof of the ill effects of untrammelled industrialization. Leeds benefited from industrialization, though, becoming a magnet for the poor seeking work, creating wealth for a nation growing prosperous as its own technical prowess and political might expanded. As early as 1812, locomotives had begun hauling coal into the city. Factories began springing up to take advantage of this cheap form of power and its attendant expansion in productivity. By 1818 there were more than 100 wool mills employing 10,000 workers. Later in the century, wool gave way to clothing production and the manufacture of heavy machinery and weapons. The city economy diversified dramatically, as did the income gap between wealthy proprietors of the new factories and those who worked in them. A 1905 study of wealth in England by Leo Chiozza, *Riches and Poverty,* estimated that the upper class – that aristocracy of title and land – amounted to 5 per cent of the country's population; the so-called middle class of shopkeepers and rising professionals accounted for 15 per cent. The "lower" or working class represented a full 80 per cent of the population, divided between the relatively comfortable skilled craftsmen and the vast unskilled labourers who lived in poverty. Such figures easily applied to Leeds.

Unfortunately, as the city became more prosperous, it could not keep up with the population growth, and the poorer classes suffered every few years from bouts of deadly cholera and other diseases. Clean water was rare and the air was polluted by the smoke from the coal-burning steam engines that powered the factories. Yet still the poor came, from Ireland, Scotland and Wales in particular, to get the jobs that, though paying poverty-level wages, were still better than what they left behind.

Somerville's father was among them. Charles Somerville was a lowland Scot who was drawn to Leeds by the plentiful work. Though not a Catholic himself (he converted years after their marriage), he married Sarah, a woman of Irish Catholic descent who practised her faith with devotion. Charles found work in a toy factory as an unskilled labourer and, despite his low wages, he and his wife embarked on a life that would include 12 chil-

dren. Henry was the second born, but the death of the first
meant that Henry would always fill the role of eldest child in the
Somerville clan.

There is little written to tell the tale of this large Irish-Scots
family. Somerville was a prolific writer, but his forte was political
and economic journalism. Personal memoirs or diaries were not
his style. Later, as the busy editor of *The Catholic Register*, he loved
to talk about big issues of faith and society. But he was largely
silent on his own personal life. Hence we know little directly
about the life of the Somervilles. What we do know, however, is
how the poor lived in their England. And the Somervilles were
certainly among them.

In those dying days of the nineteenth century, it was typical
for a working-class family of five or six to have to live on 45
shillings a week. This often included any money earned by the
wife or children who were able to work outside the home. Indeed,
family need forced Henry Somerville to leave school at the age of
13 to work in the toy factory to help support his parents and ten
siblings. At one point, he escaped the child labour inspector by
hiding on the storage shelves during inspection because his poor
family needed the "sweated wages," writes Canadian historian
Jeanne Beck in her 1977 doctoral dissertation on Somerville's
thought, *Henry Somerville and the Development of Catholic Social
Thought in Canada: Somerville's Role in the Archdiocese of Toronto,
1915–1943.*

Social historian François Bédarida reports in *A Social History
of England 1851–1975* that, of that typical 45-shilling wage,
almost half was spent on food – mostly bread and potatoes, with
eggs and a small amount of meat added for flavour. Fruit and vegetables, fish, and such treats as coffee or chocolate were rare.
Housing, including rent, heating and lighting, consumed another
seven or eight shillings. The remaining 17 shillings went to cloth-

ing, repairs, beer and tobacco (even the poor had some small consolations for their condition), insurance, outings and family amusements. Accidents were dreaded as even the smallest one could propel the family into destitution.

No wonder this was the age of the public house, [muses Bédarida]. Wasn't drink the easiest, the most universally accessible way to forget, to escape from grinding poverty, gloomy streets and squalid housing? Beer consumption, on the increase ever since the earliest days of Queen Victoria, reached a record figure at the end of the century – about three pints a day per adult male.

Where did the poor live in Leeds? Not surprisingly, there were slums, usually near the industrial districts. By the early part of the nineteenth century, the flight to the suburbs, such as they were, had already begun, leaving the poor to cram into deteriorating inner-city dwellings known as back-to-backs, tiny structures built in the back gardens of long, narrow thirteenth-century housing and commercial properties that still lined some of the central streets of Leeds. These neighbourhoods often housed some 80 to 90 people per acre. The units were cramped, often with only two rooms (a living room that doubled as a kitchen and one bedroom). By 1900 there were about 70,000 of these accommodations in the centre of the city. Family tradition has it that the Somerville home was a little better: a small, two-storey dwelling with the downstairs divided into two sections and a small room upstairs. Still, their poverty was such that there were not enough chairs to go around, so some members of the family would eat standing. The home was heated by a fireplace, which likely burned coal.

Among the poor, a disproportionate number had come from Ireland. They had in common their dire circumstances and their devotion to the Roman Catholic Church. Their foreignness, reli-

gion (still suspect to most Britons) and apparent backwardness
meant that they remained segregated from the rest of Leeds society. British society looked upon the Irish as hopelessly supersti-
tious, prone to drunkenness and unwilling to better themselves
through education. It didn't matter that the Irish had fallen into
these stereotypes largely as a result of employment patterns; they
lacked the skills necessary for more sophisticated engineering jobs
and the new jobs being created in the factories required brawn
and stamina, but little else. These Irish, shocked by a hostile anti-
Catholic culture and a new industrial society, turned inward,
looking to their own community for comfort and support.

The Catholic Church in Leeds grew in importance as the Irish
community grew in size. The Catholics originally worshipped in
private houses but began building small churches in the early
nineteenth century, as their numbers grew and anti-Catholicism
in England slowly faded. Leeds became the seat of a Roman
Catholic diocese, marked by the handsome cathedral of St. Ann.

Yet the immigrant Irish population represented only one
strand of Catholicism in England. Better known, perhaps, though
much smaller in numbers, is that privileged class of ancient
Catholic families who had for centuries remained attached to
Rome despite the Reformation, in the face of lethal persecution
from the state and English society. They were either of noble
blood (Lord Acton, the liberal historian, comes to mind) or landed gentry and thus had the protection of their wealth. Allied to
them were famous upper middle-class Anglican converts such as
John Henry Cardinal Newman and Henry Wilberforce. They were
an intellectual force in both religious and secular thought in
England far beyond what their numbers would warrant, especially in theological, literary and educational issues. Though
Somerville could never imagine himself among their number, or
even sympathize with many of their positions, their ideas never-

theless were a significant part of his own intellectual milieu as he grew into manhood.

Somerville was more directly shaped by his own social circumstances and the intellectual movements they spawned. Considering the desperate working and living conditions in Leeds, it is no surprise that it also became a focus for the rise of unions and the labour movement on the political front. The great British labour historian E.P. Thompson observed in his classic, *The Making of the English Working Class*, that as early as the late 1700s, a working-class ethos was beginning to develop in Leeds. Sympathy for the French Revolution of 1789 found a home there, and small groups gathered in secret, sharing secret oaths and plotting mischief against the property owners. The prohibited "Black Lamp" societies sprang up to promote solidarity among these proto-workers, despite the efforts of local authorities to stamp them out. These were the days when the vote was still the preserve of a small group of aristocracy and landed gentry; membership in unions was a crime on the level of treason. Yet this didn't stop working-class agitation. It wasn't unusual in mid-century Leeds for police armed with bayonets to be called out to break up riots.

By the time Somerville was born, Leeds, like all of England, enjoyed far more freedoms for its working classes, though economic freedom was not among them. Unions were by then legal and there was a lively public debate in newspapers, public houses, various high-brow journals and even in the town square of any number of ideas about how to better order the world. Marxist ideology and its many offshoots were beginning to find a ready ear, not only among the intellectuals of the universities, but also among an increasingly literate working class. The national consensus in favour of liberal, laissez-faire economics and rule by an enlightened, educated upper class was beginning to crumble.

Indeed, Bédarida called the period from 1880 to 1914 the "golden age of English socialism."

There was Marxist socialism, with the Social-Democratic Federation, founded in 1884, as its main support; there was Fabian socialism, the Fabian Society having also been founded in 1884; and there was religious socialism, as the Christian socialism of 1848 had a vigorous revival at the end of the century. On the labour side there was the Independent Labour Party, created in 1893, which acted as a link between the advanced wing of trade unionism and the elements of the middle class won over to the liberation of the workers; and there was revolutionary "syndicalism" whose forceful thrusts began in 1910.

It was a cacophony of ideas that the young Somerville faced as he became a young man. The Fabian Society, the vehicle of reformers Sydney and Beatrice Webb and playwright George Bernard Shaw, promoted the fledgling social sciences to find research to be used as propaganda tools for their mild socialism. The Labour Party itself vacillated between radical socialism and communism, which called for violent revolution, and more practical movements to better working conditions. In this arena of rising class consciousness, traditional religion suffered even more than it had earlier in the nineteenth century, when it was bruised and battered by a triumphant liberalism. Outright atheism was now not only countenanced but promoted as a rational option with its own evangelists. Liberalism, with its virtues of tolerance and respect for other opinions, was itself under attack by these more virulent and violent philosophies.

This, then, was the Leeds and the England that formed young Somerville. His fate was not to be its apologist, but its challenger. He was to enter into adulthood fiery and passionate, and remain that way for the rest of his life. Yet his preparation for this intellectual battle was not the usual route found in England: a good public school education followed by Oxford or Cambridge. Instead, he became the stereotype of the self-taught individual. School for Somerville began at age three and ended at thirteen, when he started working in the factory, like many of his friends and neighbours. While his youthful peers would accept their lot in life, Somerville did not leave the books behind in the classroom. According to his obituary, written by his brother, Charles, a Jesuit, Somerville had been a good student and a frequent visitor to the public library, where he devoured books. In fact, he often brought his books to the factory, where he would pore over them during breaks when the machinery failed.

> Though always a good Catholic boy, [Charles Somerville recalled], he was not more than ordinarily pious, but he was intensely interested in Catholic doctrine and history, especially controversy with non-Catholics. He was fascinated by all controversies and never failed to read the correspondence columns of publications where argumentative letters were included. When he was in his teens, there was an active propaganda of atheism by open-air speakers in parks and other public places. Henry listened to these speakers and was stimulated to search for the answers to their arguments. A good deal of his pocket money was spent on pamphlets of the Catholic Truth Society.

Soon he was to find that the pamphlets of the Catholic Truth Society, though handy, were not big enough weapons for the kind of battles he saw ahead. Some heavier ordnance was required.

Educating Henry

In 1908, at age 17, Henry Somerville joined the Independent Labour Party and later that year founded the Catholic Socialist Society. It was a trifle rude and audacious, bringing together 15 members from among the Catholic working class, of whom all were uneducated and some of whom were even illiterate. They unabashedly criticized the anti-socialist tirades of Catholic clergy, attracting coverage in secular and Catholic newspapers. Their audacity caught the attention of the local bishop who, without warning, condemned the group from the pulpit and in a pastoral letter.

Somerville, still young, zealous and a bit naive, was hurt and confused by this cool reception from the official Church. Yet he accepted it and resigned from the political party and his own society. He also likely felt a bit under-armed for this battle, having only his elementary school background and personal reading for an education. It was a tough but necessary lesson. The self-directed education Somerville treated himself to at the local public library during his teens had given him a taste of the exotic intellectual life lying just beyond his reach, but it had been too superficial to provide the solid foundation he needed to embark on what he began to see as his own future: serving the Church in a crusade against atheistic socialism. He wanted both to save the working class for the Church, and to save the Church for the working class.

Somerville had decided that lay obedience to the Church hierarchy trumped his own schemes for a Catholic-flavoured socialism. Still, he continued to believe privately that the Church and socialism were not mutually exclusive. To prove it, he vowed to study economics and theology, the better to arm himself intellectually so he could persuade the clergy that he was not a dangerous heretic. In fact, his ideas were natural consequences of *Rerum Novarum* [On the Condition of Workers], the famous 1891 encyclical of Pope Leo XIII that laid the groundwork for Catholic social teaching.

His rebuff by the official Church called for a change in tactics. As historian Jeanne Beck explains, he joined with Jesuit Father Theodore Evans to form the first study club for Catholic working men in England. They began meeting in 1908 at Sacred Heart Church in Leeds and agreed on several objectives: to deepen their commitment to their religion; to study economics and political theory to gain a better understanding of their modern, industrial world; and to apply Catholic social teaching to their own problems.

The timing for this initiative was opportune. It coincided with the emergence of a small but growing group of Catholic intellectuals educated at Oxford and Cambridge. (In 1895, the Church hierarchy had given Catholics permission to attend these universities.) Among them were doctors, lawyers, writers and economists. There were also young priests who were working in inner-city parishes, professional theologians and members of some religious orders who were a little less timid than the bishops when it came to challenging traditional Church attitudes. The Jesuits, in particular, played a leading role in Catholic social reform in continental Europe and were beginning to make their mark in England. They were not alone in Christian circles; their Protestant counterparts were busy in other Christian reforming movements. But the Catholics found their theological foundation in papal encyclicals and the inspiration of Henry Edward Cardinal Manning (1808–1892). Manning, an Anglican convert to the Church of Rome, had been widely admired in his later years as a tireless advocate of the rights of the poor and the working class; he was even reported to have had an influence on the writing of *Rerum Novarum.*

A year after Somerville's aborted attempt to found a Catholic Socialist Society, this like-minded group created the Catholic Social Guild in Manchester at the annual meeting of the Catholic Truth Society, a well-respected and theologically safe organization devoted to defending the faith and teaching the laity about Church doctrine. Being articulate and well-educated, they became influential in Catholic circles, including that in which Somerville circulated.

Among them was Monsignor Henry Parkinson, rector of Oscott Seminary. A pioneer in seminary education, he developed courses in social studies and advocated for the creation of inexpensive popular manuals to instruct Catholic laity in economics, social problems and the Church's social teachings.

Another was Jesuit Father Charles Plater, an Oxford graduate who believed strongly in social reform. He had been exposed to the Jesuits' work in continental Europe, where they had successfully negotiated the Vatican's obstacle course and created social policies that would not be condemned as heretical. Father Plater adapted a form of workers' retreat that was common on the continent to the English experience, hoping to bring back to the Church those men who had been alienated by its incomprehension of their industrial experience. He was to become the most significant mentor in Somerville's life.

It was Father Plater's idea to form the Catholic Social Guild and it received the bishops' approval at the meeting. The group quickly got organized, drawing up a constitution, organizing men's study groups and giving lectures. According to Beck, they also began publishing annual handbooks on Catholic social action groups in England.

Somerville was present at the official kick-off for the Guild, held in July 1911 at the first National Catholic Congress in Leeds. It was there that Father Evans introduced him to Father Plater. Father Plater quickly recognized the intelligence and determination of this young Catholic layman, who had both communications skills and first-hand knowledge of the factory floor. He encouraged Somerville to leave the toy factory and found him a job as a sub-editor of a Catholic weekly newspaper in Manchester.

If the 21-year-old Somerville had an Achilles heel, it was his lack of formal education. To rectify this situation, Father Plater found an anonymous donor who financed Somerville's enrolment in an 18-month residential program in social science at Ruskin College, Oxford. He graduated in May 1913, receiving his diploma "with distinction."

Somerville seized this opportunity in the classroom, focusing his studies on socialism. He became convinced that Leo XIII's arguments in *Rerum Novarum* provided ample refutation of socialism, but that these points were not being taught to Catholic laity, particularly to the working class. He also confirmed his suspicions that the arguments being used by English clergy to battle socialism were not only wrong, they were damaging to the Church's cause. He later wrote:

> I have confirmed by early impressions that the 'Socialism-means-Atheism-and-Free-Love' type of argument is most mischievous. Catholic and other working men are now educated enough to know that Socialism means the State ownership of the means of production; and working men are clear headed enough to know that though...it may mean many unpleasant things, it does

not mean necessarily promiscuous sexual relations or the abolition of religious worship.

Leo XIII's landmark encyclical proved to be one of the most important Church documents in existence for Somerville's evolving thinking on social questions. *Rerum Novarum* insisted that the right to privately own property was solidly based on natural law principles as well as Scripture, and it condemned those attacks on property rights by socialists. At the same time, Leo XIII broke new ground for the Catholic Church by taking up the cause of workers' rights, demanding that employers pay them a wage that allowed them to live in dignity and raise a family. The encyclical accepted the role of the emerging workers' unions, though it cautioned against socialist influences in many of them and urged governments to accept the place of Catholic workers' associations. The pope also urged governments to accept their responsibility to protect workers' rights and stamp out dangerous, unhealthy or undignified working conditions.

Armed with his newly minted diploma, Somerville had hoped to be hired as a full-time organizer for the Catholic Social Guild. Alas, the Guild was short of funds, so the young journalist kept his day job at the weekly newspaper, supplementing his income with freelance writing for other Catholic publications, until he found a job as a sub-editor at the famous liberal newspaper, the *Manchester Guardian*. On the side, he lectured and organized study groups for the Guild, getting reimbursed only for his expenses.

These lectures attempted to turn the forbidding academic language of the Church encyclicals into everyday English, the kind employed by the vast majority of the working-class Catholics that the Catholic Social Guild was trying to reach. As Beck explains:

His effectiveness as a popular lecturer and writer [was] evident in the first talks which he had delivered to the working men in 1913. The eight manuscripts of these which are still extant illustrate how he translated the formal, academic phraseology of official Church documents into brief, clear outlines of doctrine. The same ideas were presented to the Catholic intelligentsia in his journal articles and their polished continuity presented a marked contrast to the pedantic obscurantism which characterized much Catholic writing in this period.

Time after time, Somerville took up the twin themes of natural rights and the mutual responsibility of one individual to society. Drawing on Catholic doctrine, he argued that humankind had rights simply because they were human: rights to life, to marriage, to worship, to work with dignity. These did not come from the state and so could not be taken away by the state. Even in a democracy, a majority had no right to infringe on these individual rights. Somerville noted how socialists were often too eager to ride roughshod over these rights for the sake of the common good of the whole society. But if this disdain towards individual rights was the mortal sin of the socialists, those laissez-faire liberals that Somerville called "individualists" were equally guilty of another sin: ignoring the Church's principle of social stewardship. This principle taught that God supplied the natural universe for the benefit of all the earth's creatures, including humanity. Therefore, the human race could not simply do as it pleased with nature's bounty, but had to use it responsibly, ensuring that it was shared equally based on everyone's needs.

An important corollary was the "living wage," defined by *Rerum Novarum* as enough to allow the lowest-paid worker to be able to afford a life with dignity, including decent housing, enough food and clothing, and some healthy pastimes. Somerville followed a middle path between the socialist insistence that the worker-capitalist relationship was inherently oppressive of the worker and the capitalist dogma that a contract was a contract and any worker who agreed with the working conditions at the start of a job had to abide by them, no matter how impoverishing they were. To Somerville, capitalism was not necessarily unjust, but individual contracts and some types of working conditions certainly were.

As for the right to private property, anathema to socialists, Somerville found that it worked only when ownership was widely spread among many individuals and that it was balanced by responsible Christian stewardship.

His arguments sound commonplace today, almost a century later and close to 40 years after the Second Vatican Council. But at the time, they were a refreshing challenge to the conventional wisdom. Together, they formed a cohesive framework for a social policy that, though founded on Catholic social teachings, could be applied to the larger secular society. Somerville recognized that these arguments were basic principles that could be met through various strategies. He noted that no political party held a monopoly on such policies and that Catholics could in good conscience disagree on the best way to implement them. They could also use the principles to draft their own action plans, based on the philosophical bent of whatever political party they supported.

Somerville firmly believed that the Catholic minority in England could be "leaven in the yeast" of British society. If only they knew the teachings of their own Church! If Catholics would organize and study Church social encyclicals, "they could move mountains…. It may not be possible to banish all sin and suffering from the world, but…[it] would be practicable to get rid of social, as distinct from individual injustice," Somerville predicted in one of his many speeches as a young firebrand Catholic.

Together, Catholics could work to abolish indecent housing, oppressive and unsafe working conditions, poverty-level wages. They could also challenge other "reform" schemes that, in his view, were cures worse than the disease they sought to heal. Still, he insisted that differences of opinion on tactics should not stop Catholics from working together with other like-minded minorities. "Let us not then be afraid to co-operate with the heathen whenever possible," he instructed.

By 1914, the Catholic Social Guild's educational initiative had yielded some fruit. Its cheap pamphlets and organizing efforts had helped create enough interest among the Catholic community in England to spark the creation of 100 study groups with 1,500 members, according to the *Catholic Social Year Book, 1914.* These Catholics studied social and political history and economics. They were given reading lists and detailed instructions on curriculum and even how to conduct meetings. Somerville insisted that history texts be prime sources, convinced as he was that a knowledge of the past was essential for understanding the present.

The work of the Guild carried on with the support of some of the English hierarchy, most notably Francis Cardinal Bourne. As Archbishop of Westminster, he urged lay Catholics and clergy to turn to the Guild for help in understanding their role in modern society. Such support was not unanimous in the hierarchy, however, and Somerville found himself in a battle to persuade Britain's Catholics that they must leave behind their ghetto mentality and work within the larger society. Cardinal Bourne himself pitched in, arguing in a 1913 speech to the National Catholic Congress in Plymouth that, "whatever might be the case in countries where the bulk of the population was Catholic, in England the only way that Catholics could gain influence in any great movement was to participate directly in it."

In 1910, before he was named cardinal, Bourne attended a Eucharistic Congress in Montreal, where he met Archbishop Neil McNeil, then ordinary for Vancouver. The two primates hit it off, sharing opinions on the Church's mission in society and its need to co-operate with others. Bourne visited Vancouver after the congress, presiding at Mass at the cathedral and giving public speeches. No doubt he also filled McNeil in on all the activity of the Catholic Social Guild. This meeting would have an important role to play in Somerville's future.

As tensions mounted in the pre-war years, English society was wracked with social unrest, particularly with a wave of strikes from 1911 to 1913 in the trades, including taxi drivers, bakers, miners, dock workers and construction workers. Somerville was gloomy about the prospects for social peace in the climate of class hostility.

> The present situation is indeed an evil one [he wrote in an article on the labour disputes]. To a Catholic the worst aspect of the problem is not the physical suffering caused by the strikes and lockouts, but the class bitterness and ill-will engendered. Yet the present temper of the working classes, with all its evils, is to be preferred to a hopeless acquiescence in the prevailing conditions of social injustice.

By summer 1914, he concluded that revolutionary unrest was more widespread than at any time since 1848. A wide menu of schemes of social reform was offered to a discontented public. Socialists, Marxists, Syndicalists and a group called Distributionists (promoted by Catholic intellectual Hilaire Belloc) hawked their ideological wares in the chaotic politics of pre-war England. Yet all their schemes were swept aside by a much stronger force: nationalism. As the British accepted that war was inevitable, public opinion united in patriotic fervour to beat the Germans. The same phenomenon occurred in continental Europe as the socialist movements of the other belligerents in France, Germany, Russia and Italy rallied behind their governments to increase war production. Somerville saw in this situation the weakness of the socialist panaceas, but predicted that worker unrest would rise again after the war. "We shall feel the pinch when the loans have to be repaid....[a]nd when the multitudes of men now with the colours come back and glut the labour market," he wrote in the article "Socialism and the War." Somerville foresaw that the workers would turn not to the socialist parties but to the more moderate Labour Party.

Somerville knew that England's experience with the Industrial Revolution was not unique. Because both socialism and Catholicism were international, he believed they would be engaged in ideological conflict around the industrialized world, wherever the problems of modern industrial society were not being resolved by existing political structures. Catholics around the world must be prepared for the struggle, he believed. Hence, on the eve of war in Europe, he turned his back on England and headed towards its largest colony: Canada.

Canada Beckons

"Commencing salary $1,500. Come." Archbishop Neil McNeil of Toronto rarely wasted words; the telegram containing his job offer to Henry Somerville was a typical example. Somerville's reply was equally laconic. Upon arrival at the archbishop's palace on Toronto's Wellesley Place in November 1915, the luggage-bearing Briton announced, "Your Grace, I have come from England." If the archbishop was surprised, he didn't let on. The rather short but rugged Canadian cast an appraising blue eye down on the even shorter (5'4"), positively skinny young man from England. "How old are you?" he asked with a hint of doubt in his voice. Somerville must have satisfied the archbishop that he was indeed all of his 26 years, despite the boyish looks. For from that terse greeting began a long and immensely fruitful relationship that changed the Canadian Church in the twentieth century, preparing the Catholic population intellectually to take its proper place in public affairs throughout the English-speaking provinces.

The archbishop had been seeking an expert in the Church's social teachings to help him broaden the outlook of the Catholics in his charge since he took over the see of Toronto three years earlier. He had been impressed by England's Francis Bourne, Archbishop of Westminster, whom he had met in Montreal in 1910. The two prelates discovered they had much the same vision for what they believed was a necessary modernization of the Church, particularly relating to social doctrine. When McNeil was moved to Toronto, no doubt he recalled Bourne's positive descriptions of Catholic social action in England, and was

prompted to turn to the mother country to find a likely source of
the expertise he believed Toronto so desperately needed.

McNeil was a resourceful man whose long service to the
Canadian Church from coast to coast had provided him with a
wealth of contacts. He turned to one of them, his old friend Dr.
James Tompkins of St. Francis Xavier University in Antigonish,
Nova Scotia, for help in finding the right candidate. Tompkins
was conveniently on his way to England for a business trip. "Look
for a man who can come here to Toronto and promote social
studies in the interest of the working class," was McNeil's brief
request. Tompkins made his enquiries and came back with the
name of Henry Somerville, who was then working as a sub-editor
at the *Manchester Guardian*. The archbishop wasted no time getting in touch with the young journalist.

The matter-of-fact execution of this hunt for the right man,
not to mention the anticlimactic first meeting, was vintage
McNeil. For 22 years, the first Canadian-born prelate of Toronto's
Catholic Church was to bring to the diocese a penchant for
expending few words – and wasting little time – in an energetic
pursuit of his goals. His task was to steer the diocese through one
of the country's most tumultuous eras: the First World War, the
Roaring Twenties (with its influx of largely Catholic immigrants
from eastern and southern Europe), and the first years of the
Great Depression. Historians have traced the birth of Canadian
nationalism to these years, as a young nation of immigrants
adapted to their new land, with its surfeit of geography, and to
each other's different cultures. The original First Nations and the
founding French and English races, which had soon been followed in the 1800s by Irish and Scots, were rapidly being joined
by Poles, Ukrainians, Italians and Germans. McNeil was fully
aware of the momentous changes facing his flock, and equally
mindful of the cultural and economic revolution that was result-

ing from the rapid industrialization sweeping Canada and the
United States.

McNeil had served a long apprenticeship for this final task of
his career. Born in 1851 in the Cape Breton, Nova Scotia, village
of Hillsborough to parents of Scottish stock – members of the
famous Barra McNeil clan – he learned from an early age that all
work, whether it was done with the hands or the mind, was noble.
In his early years as a priest he astonished parishioners with his
finesse at the blacksmith's forge and his capacity for manual
labour. When Bishop McNeil later announced plans to build a
church, as the members of his mission parishes in the diocese of
Grand Falls, Newfoundland, would discover, he meant it literally.
Not only did he plan the church, raise money, and organize its
construction, he was often found on the roof or scaffolding, ham-
mer in hand.

Yet he was also a scholar, studying at St. Francis Xavier (St.
F.X.) in Antigonish and later doing doctoral work in philosophy
and theology at the Pontifical Urban College in Rome. A subsequent year was spent studying math and astronomy at the
University of Marseilles in France. He would start his career
teaching at St. F.X., where he served as rector for several years
before turning to parish work. An interesting sideline was journalism; besides his work with the college, he spent four years editing a small but feisty weekly Catholic newspaper called *The
Aurora*. His own views on education and the rights of fishermen
and other Nova Scotia workers, expressed in pithy and combative
prose, often stirred up local controversies. After *The Aurora* fold-
ed in 1885, he wrote for and edited *The Casket*, an Antigonish
weekly with Catholic underpinnings. The experience confirmed
his belief that the Church needed its own newspaper in order to
ensure that its views and beliefs were accurately expressed in pub-

lic debate. He would find such an outlet in *The Catholic Register* when he came to Toronto.

McNeil would become the first bishop of St. George's (Newfoundland) before being appointed to the archdiocese of Vancouver. But he only spent two years on the west coast before receiving his appointment to Toronto, which he accepted reluctantly, believing that his work in Vancouver had only just begun. McNeil was to keep the Vatican waiting almost six months before he finally took up his new duties.

As an outsider, Toronto's seventh bishop was able to bring a fresh eye to the problems of a rather inward-looking Catholic community. He was sure Toronto would benefit from new ideas that were shaping the Church throughout the world; he would bring to the city not just Somerville but also others with the talent and determination to challenge old ways of doing things, whether it was at the Catholic newspaper, at St. Augustine's Seminary or in Catholic education generally. McNeil astutely saw that the city and the diocese had to break out of a certain smugness that marred its reputation throughout Canada. As author George Boyle noted in his biography of the archbishop, *Pioneer in Purple*, Toronto was vitally important to Canada as its second-largest city, after Montreal. "It was the commercial centre of Ontario, the dominant English-speaking province of the nation," Boyle wrote. "It was a religious and educational Mecca, a centre of politics, of publishing and of the arts and letters."

However, he added,

Its reputation with the rest of the country – one must add – was generally bad, rightly or wrongly. Toronto lived in an ivory tower of its own importance. From nowhere else emanated so steady a stream of narrow and partisan views – and often in print. To the rest of the country, Toronto was so busy discovering the mote in the eye of Quebec and others that it could not find the beam in its own.

When, decade after decade, it was becoming natural for English-speaking Canadians from coast to coast to look to a great cosmopolitan centre that they might call their own, they seemed to see in Toronto a spirit of aloofness and division. Wherever lay the fault, that was the city. While his post of duty was in another realm – and would reach far beyond the limits of the Queen City – Archbishop McNeil could not live oblivious to this.

Significantly, Toronto's reputation had been earned largely by its Protestant English and Scottish majority. By contrast, the Catholic minority suffered from an inferiority complex shaped by a number of factors, including its own relatively small size; the lack of education of so many of its members (many of whom were Irish immigrants) and their working-class status; and the some-times overt disdain, or at best civil tolerance, in which they were held by the majority. Though by 1915 these conditions were rap-idly fading into history – for Catholics had come to permeate every social stratum and profession – the myth of the Irish ghetto persisted. In that year the archdiocese comprised 70,000 Catholics in the City of Toronto proper and the surrounding countryside extending east to include Oshawa, west and south to the Niagara Peninsula and north to Georgian Bay. In this predominantly Edwardian English city, new parishes were springing up regularly to serve the new communities of Italians and Poles and the mid-dle-class neighbourhoods that were sprouting around the old city. Thanks to the war effort, Toronto was rapidly industrializing and was beginning to experience all the social ills associated with a rapid immersion into the Industrial Revolution.

The Great War, 1914–1918, had another decisive impact on Toronto, beyond the fact that so many of its brightest and best young men were killed in the muddy battlefields of Europe. The bloodying in the war instilled in Canada, and particularly in Toronto, a sense of maturity as it began to accept its responsibility on a global stage and its place as a full partner in the British Empire. The war experience, by bringing together so many men from Canada's diverse racial groups, helped to shape a new pan-Canadian identity. For Canadian historian Mark McGowan, the war also affected English-speaking Catholics in a significant way, marking "a fitting climax of three decades of Catholic integration into Toronto's socio-economic fabric."

In Canada, the war effort was marred by the historic struggle between Canada's English- and French-speaking populations – this time, over the issue of conscription into the armed forces. According to McGowan, the Catholic Church, which was then still largely centred in francophone Quebec, was distrusted by many non-Catholic Canadians. It didn't help that many French Canadians felt alienated from the war effort and were often accused of disloyalty, and that Catholics in other countries, notably the Irish in the United States, Ireland and Australia, were vocal in their opposition to the war effort. Surrounded by a hostile and suspicious non-Catholic population in Toronto, the local Catholic community went to great lengths to assure their fellow citizens of their loyalty to the British Crown and of their generosity in the war effort.

In Toronto, Catholics enthusiastically endorsed the war effort and sustained their participation throughout the conscription crisis [McGowan writes in *Catholics at the Gathering Place*].

The hierarchy and clergy justified the war in religious terms and took great pains to encourage recruitment, bond purchases, and national registration. Even more striking, however, was the response of 'the common

Catholics' in the pew, whose recruitment patterns generally defied any correlation with the erratic behaviour of Toronto's economy during the war.... Above all, the First World War provided an opportunity for the Catholics of Toronto – both clerical and lay – to demonstrate proudly their love for Canada and the Empire. Their participation, both in the trenches and in the campaigns on the home front, marked the culmination of a decades-long process of integration into Canadian society and an effort to come to terms with the English-speaking Protestant Canada without surrendering their Catholicity.

In this city – English Canada's young, upstart capital – McNeil foresaw four main tasks for himself. First, he had to put the young St. Augustine's Seminary (founded in 1913) on a firm theological and financial footing. Second, he had to find money to support the building of churches in his rapidly expanding diocese. Third, he must continue the ongoing battle to protect the constitutional right of Catholics in Ontario to have their own elementary school system and expand it into secondary school. Fourth, he had to encourage the Catholic community to act quickly and contribute generously to the war effort in order to preserve good relations with the Protestant minority. He believed that if these two communities could overcome their longstanding hostility towards each other, they would serve as a model to help heal relations between French and English Canadians.

Finally – and most significantly, for Somerville – McNeil voiced his lifelong concern about the conditions of working-class Canadians. He had seen how the Industrial Revolution, with its mass-production techniques and large, dehumanizing factories, was making it difficult for working-class men and women to find employment that allowed them to retain some semblance of human dignity and afford a decent standard of living. McNeil took the Church's social doctrines seriously and advocated on behalf of workers' rights long before he came to Toronto. He believed part of the long-term answer for poorer Catholics lay in helping educate them in modern economics, history and politics and how these related to Church teaching.

To that end, he gave Somerville an official position as adviser on current affairs and lecturer on social science for St. Augustine's. Somerville was also to write a weekly column for the diocese's Catholic newspaper, then called *The Catholic Register and Canadian Extension*. This eight-page broadsheet was owned by the Catholic Church Extension Society, the evangelizing arm of the English-speaking Church in Canada, and was, for all intents and purposes, under the wing of the archbishop. Though founded in 1893 as a Catholic newspaper that would eschew the old Irish nationalist battles that engulfed the Toronto Catholic community in the late nineteenth century, *The Catholic Register* continued to carry plenty of news from Ireland. Under the editorship of Monsignor A.E. Burke, it carried on a stormy battle with non-Catholics and even those Catholics who didn't share the passionate editor's opinions on Irish questions. "If we speak in a half-hearted voice and in a whining and propitiatory tone as some of our faint-hearted ones want us to, who will pay attention to us and our claims?" Burke asked rhetorically in justification of his style, which was anything but half-hearted and guaranteed to make enemies for the priest-editor.

By 1915, McNeil had concluded that Burke's pugnacious journalism was not helping his attempts to build bridges to the Protestant majority, or even to the French Canadian Church. Burke resigned from his dual role as editor of *The Register* and president of the Extension Society and went off to Europe to be a military chaplain. Once again, the archbishop turned to old friends from Nova Scotia and persuaded Joseph Wall, K.C., a former editor of *The Casket*, to come to Toronto as Burke's replacement. According to Boyle, McNeil's biographer, "Archbishop McNeil's experience on *The Aurora* and *The Casket* and his understanding of the viewpoints of people of other denominations and races had given him a different outlook. He knew the power and compassion of simple truth. He would have a less belligerent journalism."

Joseph Wall would provide that more respectful journalism until his sudden death in 1918. The archbishop himself would write some of the articles, most notably question-and-answer style columns on Catholic catechism and Catholic education. Somerville's column, "Life and Labour," would help *The Register* expand its outlook to cover a host of subjects not usually found in religious publications of the time. From workers' rights to the philosophic underpinnings of Communism, to the notion of a fair wage, Somerville wrote in a clear, explanatory style that he hoped would reach the working-class Catholics he saw as his main audience.

It was not long before Somerville had made his assessment of the Church in Toronto and had prescribed what he believed was the answer to its needs on the social front. He saw that like the Catholic Church in England, the clergy of the English Catholic minority in Canada knew little and cared less about Catholic social teaching, and there was little support among the Catholic population for higher education. His prescription was also the same: a Canadian equivalent of the Catholic Social Guild, or at least its methods. For the seminarians he taught at St. Augustine's, wisdom would be found in a thorough examination of the encyclical *Rerum Novarum.* He started organizing social study groups for Catholic working men, and gave public lectures and debates on Catholic social thought. And then there was his column.

Somerville made it clear that "Life and Labour" was not a typical Church press offering. It was going to be a wide-ranging dis-

cussion of current events, examining and analyzing modern economic and political theory in a prose style accessible to "the needs
and interests and points of view of the Catholic working man."
Some of the topics he would handle were to include "the living
wage, the rights and duties of property, trade unionism, co-operation, the slum problem, socialism." The column would be profoundly religious in outlook, yet political in its raw material. It
would bring Catholic teaching to bear on numerous social problems, showing how Catholic thought and doctrine offered ways of
thinking that put human dignity before profit or simple utility.
He was evidently aware of the growing Social Gospel movement
in Canada led by such Protestant clergy as James Shaver
Woodsworth, who advocated a Christianity that acted to improve
material conditions on earth, which in turn made it easier for the
masses to consider their spiritual health. Catholics may shudder
at putting mammon before God, but Somerville insisted that the
Church "recognized the special importance of social questions in
our day." In fact, an understanding of life meant recognizing its
larger truths, as provided by faith, informed by serious study of
the social sciences. "Modern social problems are too complex to
be solved by reformers who have no better equipment than good
intentions," he quipped.

His used his column shamelessly to beat the drum for
Catholic study clubs. Some weeks, he offered a detailed instruction manual for organizing them. Other times, he explained that
they wouldn't conflict with other Catholic social organizations
such as the St. Vincent de Paul or Holy Name Societies. At times,
he battled the fear of revolution, which was all too real in early
Canadian history and was widespread among clergy, particularly
in Quebec, where the French hierarchy saw Communism and
socialism as twin spawns of the devil. In that first year, he wrote
columns on social study clubs, social study circles (a less formal

arrangement), how to conduct business at such clubs, and on the Catholic Social Guild in England. Unfortunately, Toronto Catholics were not overly interested. Study clubs didn't get off the ground and his lectures drew only polite interest. Historian Jeanne Beck describes the unanticipated problems Somerville faced:

> The Canadian response to this plea was mainly indifference, in spite of the moral and practical support given study clubs by Archbishop McNeil. An appeal to Catholic solidarity based on working-class consciousness was not realistic in a society which perceived itself as classless, or at least believed that unlimited economic and social opportunities were available to all ambitious and industrious citizens. Those Catholics who were most aware of the discrimination which blocked their economic advancement were often those who were also fearful of losing their faith through exposure to ideas outside the familiar Catholic milieu. Somerville soon realized that English-speaking Catholics in Canada were more isolated intellectually than Catholics in England and that their fears of apostasy must be identified and conquered.

> The war was also an important factor in Catholic indifference to study groups. It depleted the male work force and absorbed the physical and emotional energies of those who found employment in the munitions and supply industries. Somerville, in contrast, saw the war as a great catalyst of social change, particularly with many more women taking employment in factories. He warned that changes would come with post-war reconstruction which would affect all workers' welfare and that plans should be made now for working-class involvement in drafting some solutions to the problems which were

inevitable. His disappointment with Catholic indiffer-
ence to his fears was evident in some of his columns.

While the war effort was not part of Somerville's official brief,
he occasionally used his column to reinforce *The Register's* official
support of conscription. He described patriotism as a Canadian
virtue and even went so far as to describe service in the military as
a duty for Catholics. (He himself was not able to fight for medical
reasons.) In a June 28, 1917, column, he praised the "true public
spirit" of Canadian English-speaking Catholics who supported
conscription and criticized those who failed to do so. Most of the
time, however, Somerville was looking past the war, to a time
when Canadian Catholics would, more than ever, need to be intellectually prepared to handle the challenges of a post-war world
full of economic and political uncertainty. Faced with the lacklustre response to his study groups, he began to use his column as a
form of undergraduate seminar, introducing Canadian Catholics
to new concepts in economics and politics, weaving throughout
them his understanding of Catholic social theory to show how the
Church was definitely up to the challenge posed by modernity. He
would offer reading lists of proper books for Catholic social studies, reply to socialist arguments, explain the law of supply and
demand, give Catholic views on public ownership and the dehu-
manization of industry. At other times he would express his views
on matters particularly relating to Catholics, such as confessional
unions and social agencies. He was not overly keen on the former,
though he recognized the good work they were doing in Europe
and Quebec. He preferred that properly educated Catholic working men, steeped in the study of Church encyclicals, take on positions of leadership in secular unions. As for the latter, he complained that many Catholic social agencies were obsolete in their
practices and unprofessional in their care. To Somerville, they
needed better organization and their staff needed better training

and education. Finally, Somerville found the interreligious rivalry in Ontario not totally foreign, but every bit as distressing as the Catholic-bashing he had left behind in England. He urged co-operation with Protestants against a common enemy and lambasted Catholics for their self-imposed isolation.

Being single and a budding workaholic, Somerville had little time during the war years for anything but work. He found a little spare time to travel in the United States, where he came to admire the American Catholic Church's more extensive efforts to promote the Church's social teachings, and to lecture in Canada. For leisure, he read copiously and enjoyed long Saturday afternoon walks with Archbishop Neil McNeil, who was fast becoming a lifelong friend and mentor. The archbishop prized his walks and bragged to others about how long he could go. (He wrote to a friend in 1913 that he had walked "nine full miles without a stop.") McNeil liked to have a companion on his exercise and he often chose Somerville. The two men could walk block after block of Toronto's streets without exchanging more than a few words. But those few words, usually on an issue they were grappling with, would often find their way, in some shape or form, into one of the younger man's columns or lectures.

Though Somerville's emphasis on social conditions was a departure among early twentieth-century Catholics, as was his defence of unions, it did not make him a radical in any theological sense. It would be a mistake to paint him as a prototype of post-Vatican II reformers, who also had an affinity for social justice. Though they shared his passion for this aspect of Church teaching, late-twentieth-century Catholic social justice advocates would have found little in the rest of Somerville's beliefs to parallel their own. In other doctrinal matters, or even social attitudes, Somerville expressed either nothing at all, or views loyal to traditional Church teaching. For instance, as a well-read Catholic he would have been familiar with the Church's battle against modern historical approaches to Scripture – probably its most heated philosophical debate in the pre-war period – but he stayed away from the controversy. His concerns lay elsewhere. As Beck observes:

> Although Henry Somerville was forthright in criticizing the educational, political and social apathy of Canadian Catholics, he was not a theological or social radical in the contemporary sense. He did not seek to change, but to bring to fruition the principles which he found outlined in the magisterium of the Church. These were based on the Bible, the Church's traditions, the writings of the Doctors of the Church, particularly St. Thomas Aquinas, and most recently and urgently the papal encyclicals. He believed in a practised obedience to the hierarchy in matters of faith and morals and he eschewed theological controversy. Thus, although he was aware of the Modernist Movement, he never commented on this controversy in any of his articles or editorials. He supported the Church's opposition to such practices as birth control, sterilization of the "feeble-minded," state education for Catholics, and revolutionary socialism. He was conscientious in his observance of the Church's regulations in his personal religious practice.

For a few months, beginning in late 1917, Somerville reported for the *Toronto Star* to earn a little extra money. However, work for the Catholic Church remained more appealing and he soon left to devote himself full-time to study and writing. In May 1918, at McNeil's urging, he paid a visit to St. Francis Xavier University in Antigonish, where he had been invited to give a commencement address. It was an eminently suitable occasion, as St. F.X. was to be the birthplace of the Antigonish Movement, an offshoot of Catholic social action devoted to helping educate the farmers and fishermen of the Maritimes, founded by Father Moses Coady in the late 1920s. In the war years, under the leadership of McNeil's friend, Tompkins, it had already begun to establish its leadership in Catholic social teaching, creating "the People's School" to work with farmers and co-operatives. Somerville would prove to be a kindred spirit to the likes of Tompkins and Coady.

In Antigonish he received a welcome gift: an honorary Master of Arts degree for his work in promoting the education of Catholic working men and women. The honorary degree reaffirmed everything this mostly self-taught working-class journalist had fought for. "He was always proud of this, his only university degree, for it proved that unlimited opportunities were available for all Catholics if they were diligent," wrote Beck. The trip also offered a tantalizing prospect for the ambitious young man; he was offered a position on faculty as a professor of sociology. He accepted, arranging to take up his new duties in September, after delivering a lecture in Montreal and going on retreat at Oka, Quebec, the home of a Benedictine monastery.

But a vacation to England at Christmas, made possible by the signing of the Armistice on November 11 to signal the end of the war, interrupted his academic career before it had a chance to take off. Back in Leeds, family duties and the entreaties of his old Catholic friends persuaded him that he was needed more at home in England than in Canada. He would not return to Toronto for another 15 years.

Troubles

For the second time in Henry Somerville's life, the Atlantic Ocean would figure as both a symbolic and literal divide between the old and the new, between the pull of home and family and the ambitions represented by a life working for the pioneering Roman Catholic Church in North America. As in 1915, a steam-crossing of the cold North Atlantic would signal the end of one part of his life and the beginning of another. These passages would become a common motif in the life of the expatriate Briton.

But this one had its own unique features. Though only three years had gone by since his first ocean voyage, more than the mere passing of chronological time had occurred in the interim. These years covered one of those rare moments in history that define the end of an epoch and a departure into something altogether different. In 1915, Somerville had left an England at war; it was the heart of the mighty British Empire, the most powerful political entity on earth, and it had turned all its formidable resources to the task of defeating the Triple Axis of Germany, Italy and the Austro-Hungarian Empire. The war was still relatively young and doubts about the cost – particularly in terms of the lives of the nation's youth – were only beginning to be politely raised. Though Somerville approved of the war effort, his approval was tinged with both sadness and discomfort over how easily British society had turned into a war machine. It was a fierce and stone-faced country that he had left to come to Canada. Now, in 1918, the war was over, the armistice signed. Though officially the alliance led by England (along with significant contributions from its dominions such as Canada), France and the United States had won the war, the cost had been far higher than anyone had dreamed possible. The devastating impact of the Great War, the War to End All Wars, was felt around the globe. Europe was in ruins; even Great Britain, saved from physical destruction by the English Channel, was physically, morally and spiritually prostrate. On the map of the world, the distinctive red of the British Empire covered more of the earth's surface than it ever had. But at its core in England, the Empire was empty.

Most distressing was the death toll. Canada alone lost over 60,000 soldiers, a fraction of what the major belligerents suffered, but a significant percentage of the young men of a lightly populated nation. Britain had lost 743,000; Italy, 615,000; France, 1,384,000; Austria-Hungary, 1,290,000; Russia, 1,700,000. Germany suffered the greatest loss of life, with 1,800,000 dead. The United States, because it entered the war well after it started, had 48,000 dead. The figures were mind-numbing, the result of old military strategies that failed to account for the cold efficiency of lethal new weapons. The loss of some of the best talent of a rising generation would haunt Europe for the next two decades.

The war left chaos in its wake in Europe. Germany was in revolution as Marxist and socialist groups fought with radical conservatives for power in the nation's wounded cities. It would take another year of bloody street violence before the Weimar Republic, which took over after the resignation of Kaiser William II, could consolidate its control over the nation. Russia had already had its Communist Revolution in 1917 and had withdrawn from the war, but the end of hostilities provided an opportunity for Western countries to attempt an outside coup against the young Bolshevik regime. An international force involving British, French, American, Japanese, Baltic and Slavic soldiers invaded Russia in the hopes of helping anti-Communist Russians topple the revolutionary regime in Moscow, but the effort was short-lived as the participants soon realized that invading the world's largest landmass, especially one with the most forbidding geography and climate, was more than their exhausted forces could handle.

Ireland, too, was the source of great anxiety and more bloodshed. The Easter Rising of 1916 had been violently crushed by British forces, sent there by the British government which still governed the island nation. But sympathy for Irish nationalism had grown during the war. In January 1919, Irish nationalist members of Parliament gathered in Dublin to proclaim Ireland a republic, thus ushering in "The Troubles," a period of guerrilla-style war with British forces, followed by civil war that lasted until 1923.

Even England experienced economic upheaval and mass unemployment, which created a rising appetite for a politics of extremism. On the left side of the political spectrum, it went beyond the moderate socialism of the Labour Party, to card-carrying Communists, anarchists (not card-carrying) and revolutionaries of various stripes. Strikes broke out in different industries, leading many of Britain's conservative statesmen to suspect a co-ordinated covert attack on the nation by an international Communist conspiracy. There was such a thing. The Moscow-controlled Communist International (Comintern) was founded in 1919 for just such a purpose, though it would eventually become a simple pawn of the Russian government. And while its zealots worked feverishly for the revolution, over the years their impact was limited in the more developed industrial nations such as Britain, as workers shied away from wholesale revolution in favour of striving for better working conditions and wages.

The British people had, despite the victory celebrations in the wake of November 11, suffered psychological damage that reached far beyond the casualty lists. The meaninglessness of the war left them angry, particularly the returning veterans, who wondered what purpose there had been in their sacrifice. They found the increasing forgetfulness of those back home incomprehensible. War poet Siegfried Sassoon, in his poem *Aftermath* (March 1919), growled out the inchoate anger felt by many of the men who had fought in the trenches:

Have you forgotten yet? [...]

Look down, and swear by the slain of the War that you'll never forget.

Do you remember the dark months you held the sector at Mametz –

The nights you watched and wired and dug and piled sandbags on parapets?

Do you remember the rats; and the stench

Of corpses rotting in front of the front-line trench –

And dawn coming, dirty-white, and chill with a hopeless rain?

Do you ever stop and ask, 'Is it all going to happen again?'

Many looked fruitlessly for meaning in the four years of tragedy and found none. Some then looked for easy answers and found scapegoats. Even as Adolf Hitler, then a corporal in the German army, was beginning his long march to power by inciting hatred against the Jews of Germany, others elsewhere, even in Britain, found an outlet for their anger and fear in anti-Semitism. Many of the same people who feared the rise of the "Red Menace" in global Communism also despised the Jews. In 1919, the publication of *The Protocols of the Elders of Zion* touched off a frenzy of anti-Semitism, particularly in some members of the more right-wing popular press. Though exposed a year later as a fraudulent document dating back to Czarist Russia, this purported strategy for Jewish world domination found believers in many circles, including among the elites in the military and the government.

The desire for order, security and simple answers led to the rise of Fascism, an ideology that loosely tied extreme nationalism with elements of belief in old-fashioned virtues of strictness and obedience to family, state and, in some cases, religion. As the famous Marxist historian Eric Hobsbawm has pointed out, Fascism was not a coherent philosophy but was better defined as a sentiment of anti-Communism, anti-liberalism, racism and an intolerance for opposition. Fascist leaders such as Hitler, through his National Socialist Workers Party (Nazis), would refashion Fascism as totalitarianism, daring to dictate not just the activities but the very thoughts of Germany's citizens. Italy would carry the Fascist banner under Benito Mussolini; other countries, including England, had similar movements.

This was the state of Europe even as it celebrated the end of the war. It must have been quite a shock to the 29-year-old idealistic journalist. Somerville was coming home for a long-awaited holiday; he could be forgiven for feeling a little self-satisfied after a successful stint as newspaper columnist and lecturer in the new world. He had been widely acclaimed as a credit to the Church in Canada and had won the trust of one of its most powerful prelates, Archbishop Neil McNeil of Toronto. He had earned an honorary Master of Arts degree from St. Francis Xavier University and taken a new teaching position there. He could have reasonably expected a warm welcome from his aging but proud parents and his many siblings.

Instead of mirth and joy, Somerville was quickly immersed in gloom and disappointment. The relief and happiness over the end of the war had been quickly dissipated by the emerging economic problems and the chaos of demobilization facing the vast armies that had gathered in Western Europe. The immediate impact on

Somerville's life of the war's end was the untimely end of his teaching career. Somerville arrived in England just as every available ship was being commandeered by the victorious governments to ferry the troops back to North America. For months into the foreseeable future, there was not a spot to be found on any cross-Atlantic passage. Somerville sadly wired his superiors at St. Francis Xavier to tell them he wouldn't be returning anytime soon.

Then there were family problems. Over the holidays his mother had taken sick with pneumonia and died. This was a heavy blow for his father: a good man in his own right, but a life-long labourer who didn't feel at all well-equipped to raise the children left at home. Somerville felt he couldn't leave his father during such a crisis. He wrote to his former employer, Archbishop McNeil, in February 1919: "I am the eldest of 10 children, seven of whom are at school or college. My father, being a labouring man, with no experience of education or of the placing of young people in good positions of employment himself, wants to have me nearby in order to discuss these questions about the raising of the family."

Neither was family the only claim on him. His old friends at the Catholic Social Guild were relieved that he had returned and immediately began to pressure him to take on a position of leadership as organizing secretary. Not only did Somerville feel some sense of responsibility to the Guild, since it had helped him receive his own education some years earlier, but the proposition also aroused his sense of mission to bring Catholic social teachings to his fellow countrymen, particularly in the face of the rising challenge to the Church posed by Communism and Fascism. It held out tantalizing possibilities, even if the Guild had almost no money and few members.

Reluctantly, he determined that England needed him more than Canada – at least for the time being. It was a hard choice; he had enjoyed his time in Toronto immensely, finding the city modern and Canadians friendly, cheerful and optimistic. England seemed drab, fussy and exasperating by comparison. "After three years of Canadian life the conditions on this side do not appear to me attractive," he told McNeil in his letter. "The climate is maddening and the general arrangements of things so out of date, so lacking in order and swiftness, and the people so slow yet so struggling, that I wish myself back in Toronto with its newness, and its quickness and conveniences."

He didn't say, but he could have, that he missed his Canadian mentor. It sounds trite, but it is also true that Archbishop McNeil had been a father figure for Somerville. The journalist had quickly won the archbishop's confidence and became a trusted adviser, a sounding board and a regular guest on the archbishop's Saturday afternoon walks. So close was their relationship that Somerville was happy to sign off his letters as "Your Grace's affectionate child."

But Canada was now a long way away. And Britain, in its suffering, needed him. Fortunately, he was not without financial support. Even before leaving Canada, he had contracted with the *Toronto Star* to write articles from England on European matters during his stay. His first assignment was the Paris Peace Conference, which got underway on January 18, 1919. Bringing together all the belligerents, it took almost six months to hash out the conditions of Germany's defeat. Because of its harsh demands of war reparations and restrictions on Germany's military capabilities, the conference would sow the seeds for the Second World War a generation later, an even deadlier world conflagration beginning in 1939. Somerville jumped at the opportunity to put his journalistic skills to work on a major story and began filing other articles for the *Star* from various points in Great Britain and Europe.

More to his liking, however, was his work for the Catholic Social Guild. Somerville feared that during the war years, the Catholic Church of England would have gotten nowhere with its social doctrine. He was right. The war had decimated the Guild and ambitious plans for the group were put on hold. The study groups declined as their members went off to war or found their time consumed by the industrial war production. When the war ended, the Guild struggled unsuccessfully with English Catholic apathy. It had little money, so the first and most urgent need was for a membership and fundraising campaign. Hoping to capitalize on the enthusiasm found in previous years among Catholic intellectuals, the Guild closed its London office and moved to Oxford in the summer of 1919. Somerville became its full-time secretary-organizer, and was paid three pounds a week. In 1920, as part of the Guild's strategy to help working Catholic men understand their Church's social doctrines, Jesuit Father Charles Plater, Somerville's first mentor and friend, started a summer school at Oxford. Somerville was lecturer on contemporary social issues at this 10-day forum for workers and study club members, both men and women, many of whom were from northern industrial towns.

In January 1921, Somerville became the first editor of *The Christian Democrat*, a monthly journal published by the Guild. Father Plater died that same month at age 46, a victim of overwork and a heart condition. He was the inspiration for the Guild and the glue that held it together; for Somerville, the Jesuit priest was the most important influence in his career. Plater gave him his start, and provided a prime example of the Catholic faith in action among the poor. Somerville would miss him sorely.

Later that year, the Catholic Workers College was started at Oxford's Ruskin College, thanks largely to Somerville's efforts to rouse support, using the great goodwill that existed for his late mentor to generate the necessary funds. Three labourers enrolled in the first program; Jesuit Father Leo O'Hea was made principal. Somerville and other Guild members lectured, often free of charge. Father O'Hea and the three men, two from Lancashire and one from South Wales, lived together in a rooming house. Catholic organizations from the students' hometowns provided scholarships to cover tuition while wealthy Catholics contributed to the college's general expenses.

The college's initial success, however, also led to Somerville's departure. The Guild had incurred significant debt as the result of the purchase of a large house for its operations in Oxford. This scared the overly cautious Somerville, who saw plenty of potential for bankruptcy ahead as England struggled through the post-war depression. Believing the debt would preoccupy the Guild and deflect it from its main objectives, he opted to resign as secretary, though he continued to write for *The Christian Democrat*, lecture and help raise money. But he remained disappointed that the Guild's first important initiative, in which he had placed high hopes as a model for lay leadership in the Church, would be put into the hands of a priest.

A significant diversion during this time was a trip in the winter of 1922 to lecture at "the People's School" at St. Francis Xavier University. The school featured an eight-day study session for agricultural and industrial workers who took courses in subjects ranging from arithmetic to grammar. Somerville's contribution was a series of lectures on social science. In addition to giving talks at the school, he also lectured in Saint John, New Brunswick, in Cape Breton, and at Loyola School of Sociology in Montreal.

He also responded to a challenge from the Montreal Labour College to debate his argument that Catholic social doctrines could help the working class achieve social justice. A large, lively crowd came to hear his talk on "Religion and Labour": "It was reported with great elaboration in the daily press, and all my meetings there during the week, except private lectures in religious houses, were henceforth given generous publicity," Somerville said.

His North American tour also included a trip to Washington and New York. In the U.S. capital he met Father John A. Ryan, the famous leader of the Catholic social movement in the United States, and gave a lecture to Ryan's students at the Catholic University of America. His visit to the two most important cities in the United States led to the development of useful contacts with members of the National Catholic Welfare Council, laymen and priests who were becoming influential in U.S. labour and government circles.

As valuable as this trip would be to Somerville's future career with the Church, it did not offer much of a living. To supplement his regular income, he covered political and economic events, both major and minor, from the capital of the British Empire for the *Toronto Star* for the next 11 years. Among these was the Imperial Conference of 1923. This event was of interest to Canadian readers since their own prime minister, William Lyon Mackenzie King, would be attending. This was his first major performance on the world stage since his election in 1921; King used the occasion to confirm to the Empire that Canada would pursue an independent foreign policy. Somerville enjoyed his new job; with it came more money than he had ever earned and a certain cachet that accompanies working for a major daily newspaper, even if it was a colonial one in the eyes of the British. He was proud of his work and valued the opportunity to be an interpreter of European events for readers in Canada. In 1927, in an article in *T.P. Cassell's Weekly*, he described his job in glowing terms:

> If the London correspondent of a great overseas newspaper is the right man, he has the most fascinating and envi-

able job in the whole realm of journalism. The big news of the day is always his assignment. If it is an important debate, he is at the House of Commons. If there is a big legal action going on, he is at the High Courts. If there is a royal garden party, he is at Buckingham Palace. If there is an international crisis, he is at the Foreign Office. A representative of an English home paper is but a cog in a wheel. The London correspondent is a newspaper personality in himself. He receives the deference and the privileges due to the accredited representative of another nation.

More importantly, the steady income allowed him to think about things other than work, such as getting married and having a family. At 33, he was already slipping past the usual age for marriage and may have wondered whether marital bliss would ever be his lot in life.

He met Margaret Cecilia Cooper at the home of his boyhood friend Alec Cooper in Headingly, a working-class section of Leeds. It was the home of George and Polly Cooper, a Catholic couple with three sons and Margaret, their youngest. They were a devout and sociable family who not only enjoyed music but exhibited fair talent. George Cooper was a railwayman by trade but had an artistic side, writing poetry and playing the violin. Though his employment put him squarely in the working class, his own roots were in a landed middle-class family in Scotland. He had once studied to become a Presbyterian minister, but marriage and studies drew him to the Catholic Church and away from his Protestant family. Still, his home retained the elegance and style more familiar to the gentry than to common folk.

It was certainly a step or two up from what Somerville was used to. His own family had lived from hand to mouth, scrabbling for the next meal and a little coal for the fire. Somerville found himself drawn into the Cooper family circle through the Church.

He and other friends of the family would often be invited back to the Cooper home after church events, where they would enjoy an evening of music and mirth. There his eye was attracted to the fun-loving Margaret, a vivacious young woman who had returned home after three years as a postulant in a convent. Ill health had prevented her from taking vows. It is possible that her poor health was the result of medical malpractice during surgery to remove her appendix. Janet Somerville, Henry and Margaret's youngest child, explains:

> The family legend has it, and my mother told it over and over again so I assume it's true, that the surgeon who did that job managed to stitch her intestines closed, not completely but seriously. So, of course, she always vomited and they decided she had nervous dyspepsia and she didn't have a vocation. So I'm very glad they decided she didn't have a vocation. It wasn't until her first child, until the birth process nearly killed her, that they discovered there had been an egregious surgical error some years before.

The convent's loss would become Somerville's bride. Though he had admired her, he thought the pretty Margaret was far too young for him. He hardly spoke to her, and certainly never alone. But when he found out she was only a couple of years younger than he, Somerville decided to move fast before she was scooped up by someone else. In late January 1923, Margaret was taken aback by a letter she received in the post. It was from Somerville, and it was a marriage proposal, although that wasn't absolutely clear: someone not knowing the serious Somerville could have misconstrued the letter as a proposal for missionary work. The would-be gallant did his best to describe his lover's admirable qualities, but he was no Cyrano de Bergerac. "But what has always most attracted me to you has been your Catholic devotion," he wrote. Nor did romance figure into it; it was more of a partnership in doing God's work.

For myself, during many years I thought marriage was something to which I could not look forward. I long thought of being a priest and when I was convinced that that was not my vocation, I thought I must devote myself as a layman to work which would not permit me to marry. I have never been the Catholic I ought to be. My faults are grievous ones. But I can say with some humility that I have refused material things for God's sake and that, contemptible as I am, I have been the means of doing important work for God's Church. At the moment I am not principally engaged on Catholic work. I am doing fairly well in the way of earning money. Perhaps I would become comparatively well off if I threw myself into the effort at newspaper success. I don't think I ever will become so absorbed in newspaper work. I don't want to do so. I want to be always doing a fair amount for the Church and it may be that I may be needed some time again for full-time Catholic work. If you were sharing my life I am sure you would want me to consider the quality of the work I was doing and not simply the amount of the salary. You once offered your life completely to God and I am sure that your intention still remains in its integrity though your way of life is not what you once proposed. I have not your goodness but I love best the things you love best. I would always work with you to realize your own ideals and you would help me to be faithful to mine.

Margaret's response fairly oozed astonishment, though it was also remarkably businesslike in expressing the religious devotion her suitor had recognized.

I should like to see you when convenient to yourself. Any time will be right for me if perhaps you will let me know so that I may keep myself quite free, [she wrote on January 22]. Ever since I left Manchester [where she had been in the convent], at every Holy Communion I have offered my heart, soul and body to our Lord to do with as He pleased. I begged Him to show me which way He would like me to serve Him and then I have tried to be careful not to do anything myself which might cause me to be in any way conspicuous. Then I thought if anything was shown to me it would be God's will. Please do not think I am a holy person, with that exception I am simply teeming full of faults. Now I can't say any more. You see your letter was a very big shock and I am more like a newly wound up mechanical toy at present, moving without being able to think or feel very much.

A week later Somerville was back in Leeds. The engagement took place that weekend with the blessing of Margaret's parents. Within a short time the two finally had their moment alone, likely when they went to purchase the wedding ring, and the wedding took place before the year was out. The couple purchased a small home under construction and settled down to married life in London. Somerville settled into his work.

The *Toronto Star* provided an income, but it was his efforts on behalf of the Church that occupied his heart. Outside his day job as a newspaper journalist, Somerville remained devoted to raising the Catholic working class of England to a higher understanding of the social doctrines of the Church so that they could more effectively fight for their rights and dignity in British society. He saw the problem as fourfold: 1) presenting the Church's social doctrines most effectively; 2) deciding which political party would best represent the working class; 3) dealing with official

Catholic squeamishness over the British Labour Party, which
openly advocated "socialism," a word that was like chalk grating
on blackboards for many priests and bishops; and 4) deciding
which "socialist" party Catholics could support in good conscience. Despite his sympathies for left-wing politics, he found
that potential allies in the labour movement didn't make his job
any easier. Many union leaders were outright anti-religious and
more than a few were open Communists. Perhaps a trifle naively,
which was typical of liberals of the time, Somerville believed that
with more education about the Church's contributions to social
justice, the working class, union leaders and even politicians
would become converts to the cause and press for social reforms
based on Catholic teachings.

His mostly unpaid publishing ventures during this period
were all channelled towards this end. They included several series
of essays on economic and social history, a book on the Catholic
social movement in Europe, called simply *The Catholic Social
Movement* (published in 1933 by Burns, Oates and Washbourne),
and numerous analytical articles dealing with contemporary
problems. He also found himself lecturing from time to time at
British seminaries and colleges, including Stonyhurst, Oscott,
Wonersh and the English College in Rome.

Somerville's favourite hobby horse was to advocate using the
medieval guilds as role models for his new vision of working-
class–inspired economic reform. These guilds had been associations of artisans, such as coopers, bakers, carpenters and tailors.
By joint action, not unlike today's trade unions, members were
able to secure a decent standard of living and a comfortable position in society. Their success, he believed, was partially grounded
in their acceptance of the spiritual and moral authority of the
Roman Catholic Church. While recognizing the excesses of
Christendom, Somerville saw in the guilds' collectivist approach

to social questions a more humane way to establish economic relations than the laissez-faire capitalism of the early twentieth century. He saw a form of respect for workers shaped by the thought of St. Thomas Aquinas, the medieval philosopher/theologian and Doctor of the Church who had advocated just wages and prices. In his disdain for what he considered ruthless and anti-social individualism, Somerville was a prescient voice in the wilderness.

Being a diplomatically astute man, Somerville knew that his sympathy for Labour politics and "socialist" legislation often put him afoul of Catholic conservatives in England. In order to overcome these deep-seated suspicions of socialism, he put the most popular socialist groups through the wringer of Catholic social teaching in order to separate the rhetoric of camp followers from what British socialist leadership really stood for and attempted to accomplish. Not one to shy away from a challenge, he took on the giants of the time – George Bernard Shaw and John Maynard Keynes – and not just secular intellectuals: the Catholic literary giants Hilaire Belloc, G.K. Chesterton and Philip Snowden also went under his microscope. But he saved his closest scrutiny for the British Labour Party.

This was playing with fire. Somerville was well aware of the censure for any socialist party that was found in Pope Leo XIII's 1891 encyclical *Rerum Novarum*, which he held in the highest esteem. If the British Labour Party fit the encyclical's description of socialist, he knew Catholics would be forbidden to support it. His method was to determine whether individual policies of the party or statements of party leaders could truly be described as "socialist." He concluded that, though the party's constitution had a socialist clause in its constitution, it rejected revolutionary methods for achieving its goals. Therefore it represented a watered-down version of socialism that really wasn't all that different from Catholic social doctrine. Somerville also saw in the socialist leadership a tendency towards moderation, particularly as its chances of coming to power increased.

The British Labour Party had its roots in union expansion of the late nineteenth century. In 1900 the powerful Trades Union Congress, a coalition of many of Britain's largest unions, began supporting Labour delegates. The Labour party became an official organization in time for the 1906 election and elected 29 members to Parliament, a significant minority bloc. However, the real breakthrough for the party came during the war. As the military machines required ever-increasing amounts of weapons and ammunition, not to mention ships, planes and land vehicles of all kinds, British industry grew rapidly, accompanied by a doubling in union membership to eight million in 1919. The Labour party also reconstituted itself, developing an even closer alliance with trade unions while at the same time reaching out to new members in the wider public. This proved to be a successful formula; the party's representation in the House of Commons grew from 63 members in 1918 to 191 members in 1923, when it won a general election under the leadership of Ramsay MacDonald.

But was it "socialist" in the sense understood by the Catholic Church? That was the question Somerville pondered. According to historian R.K. Webb, MacDonald, a capable leader, was also a moderate with a keen understanding of political reality. Under his leadership, his party pursued conventional policies on the economic front, such as support for free trade and a balanced budget. Moreover, though the famous "Clause VI" of the party's constitution called for securing "for the producers by hand and by brain the full fruits of their industry, and the most equitable distribution thereof that may be possible, upon the basis of the common ownership of administration and control of each industry and service," MacDonald's government made no moves to put that principle into practice. And its pursuit of power was eminently democratic.

Its relations with Bolshevik Russia were more ambiguous. As Webb observes, British Labour supporters were rather hostile to Communists in their own backyard, even as they expressed sympathy for the Russian Revolution. While refusing to affiliate with the British Communist Party, which was founded in 1920, Labour nevertheless supported diplomatic recognition of the Soviet Union and two treaties with the successor state to old Czarist Russia.

MacDonald's British Labour Party never had a chance to prove whether its socialist rhetoric was more bite than bark. It was defeated in an election in 1924 in which anti-Communism played an important part. Nevertheless, it continued to play a significant role in British politics, though it wouldn't form another government until after the Second World War.

Athough Somerville concluded the "socialist" party was hardly worthy of the name, he didn't see it as the salvation of the British working class. Only by injecting some rigorous thinking based on Catholic social encyclicals could the party truly begin to offer workable solutions for the economic inequality of the day. But to do that, Catholics had to feel comfortable working for change within the party. This would not happen unless the Church was willing to accept the Labour Party as a legitimate expression of democracy. As historian Jeanne Beck has noted:

> With the Church's present inflexible policy, Catholics in the Party were at a great disadvantage as "it is sometimes difficult to get much consideration in the Labour Party if one does not give lip service to socialism." [Somerville] advised young Catholics to resist this temptation, and to seek the removal of the socialist label from Labour Party

policies. But his conclusion was that the party's political and economic statements and actions should not preclude Catholic support…. In effect, Somerville's defence of Catholic involvement in organizations suspect to the Church required some manoeuvring through a maze of clerical pronouncements, but he held to the principle that "the question of whether a Catholic can be a socialist…must depend mainly on what is meant by socialism."

The diminutive Somerville also found himself taking on the rather impressive figures of G.K. Chesterton and his equally famous contemporary Hilaire Belloc, but from the opposite end of the spectrum from socialism. These formidable Catholic intellectuals were promoters of a small, rather obscurantist economic sect called the Distributionists, which had come out of Belloc's understanding of Catholic social teaching. It had attracted other middle-class intellectuals after the First World War, thus causing Somerville some worry. The Distributionists were not serious economists, but attracted some attention to their eccentric form of Little Englandism, which advocated breaking the economy down into the largest number of small landowners, commercial firms and manufacturers. It was essentially a form of isolationism based on utopian notions of simpler lifestyles and the rejection of consumerism. Somerville feared the alliance of Chesterton and Belloc to these simplistic economic nostrums would tarnish the Church's intellectual reputation and reinforce common prejudices towards Catholics as backwards reactionaries. In 1927 he took on this dynamic duo, both in the press and at the lectern, declaring in *The Christian Democrat* that he must "expose the Distributionists' absurdities because they had led so many earnest-minded Catholics up a blind alley away from the broad Catholic road, that non-Catholics were taking Distributism to be a Catholic product and were scandalized thereby." As for

Chesterton, a prolific and famous orthodox Catholic convert whom Somerville admired greatly, Somerville believed he had fallen victim to his own "besetting fault of…exaggeration induced by stupendous verbal dexterity…and an…eye only for the facts that appeal to his mood and failing to see the facts in their setting." There is a family legend that Somerville even took on the great man in public debate, a popular form of public entertainment at the time. His second son, Stephen, recalls the story:

> Yes, it's true. They were on the same stage. Chesterton laughingly or mockingly referred to his "doughty opponent." Chesterton was a huge man, 6'3" and over 300 pounds; Dad was 5'4" and 110 pounds. But he was a sharp debater. Of course, Chesterton would have been, too. It would have been a really lively time.

Somerville's own analysis of society's economic ills saw twentieth-century capitalism as the root of economic oppression. Having torn apart organic society by pitting worker against management, capitalism was ensuring that even democracy was in peril because of the upper classes' stranglehold on power. He criticized common socialist solutions, however, for ignoring humanity's spiritual nature and insisting on economic remedies based on pure self-interest. He saw the worker–manager relationship as a partnership rather than a duel, one that could work for the benefit of both in industrial enterprises. He had no problem with owners making profits, as long as they were not excessive, but he insisted that workers share in the success of the company.

Somerville's ideas for a middle way between socialism and pure capitalism, a sort of modern version of the medieval guild, never caught on in Britain. But he never abandoned the notion of a "modern equivalent to the medieval principle of the just price, applying it to wages, rent, interest and profit."

In October 1929, stock markets crashed, ushering in the
Depression. As prices collapsed around the world, as inflation
made some currencies next to worthless, as unemployment
soared, social reform seemed as utopian a goal as ever. Strikes
became more common, and more bitter. To Somerville, the most
reasonable alternative to long, costly work stoppages was the arbi-
tration of labour disputes based on bargaining rights enshrined in
legislation. But the time was not right for being reasonable.
European Catholic workers were turning to more extreme solutions, particularly the socialists and Communists. In 1931, in the
heart of the Depression, Pope Pius XI issued the encyclical
Quadragesimo Anno, an update of *Rerum Novarum* adapted for a
world 40 years older, one in which social division based on class
seemed to be ever more extreme, in which the solutions of Marx
and Engels were attracting more, and more ruthless, adherents
while capitalist societies seemed blind to the social disintegration
created by a winner-take-all economic system. According to Beck,

> It was so explicit in its purpose and in the exposition of
> contemporary problems that the principles of the
> encyclical were adopted immediately as the cornerstones
> of the Church's social theory during the 1930s. They were
> of particular significance to societal reformers such as
> Henry Somerville and [American] John Ryan as they
> could be interpreted as authorization for increased
> Catholic social action.

Pius XI echoed Pope Leo XIII's teachings of 1891 and took
them several steps further. While reaffirming the teaching that
property ownership was a natural right, Pius XI noted that the
state had a responsibility to ensure that private property was used
in keeping with the common good. He urged greater collabora-
tion between labour and management, insisting that the fruits of
their enterprises be shared equitably. A working wage, he went

on, must support a labourer and his family and allow him to acquire property for a home and garden. Pius XI also took on the cult of the individual, blaming it for destroying all sense of community and co-responsibility. He was particularly scathing of the ownership class, calling it a "despotic economic dictatorship." Unfortunately for men like Somerville, Pius XI was no more accommodating towards socialism, finding that "Christian socialism" was a contradiction: "No one can be at the same time a good Catholic and a true socialist." Still, Pius XI recognized the failure of Church leaders to meet the needs of the workers and urged them to accept their responsibility for fighting for economic and social reform.

Somerville saw in this encyclical new support for his long-held views that the laity had a distinctive role to play in promoting the kingdom of God independent of the official Church. This could be done through union activism, he argued, and not necessarily Catholic unions. From 1929 to 1933, he doubled his writing activity, always pursuing his themes of economic inequality and political ineptitude towards the rights of workers.

A highlight of Somerville's career in secular journalism was a *Toronto Star* assignment to travel to Russia in the spring of 1929 to investigate the Soviet government's five-year economic plans. While his reports were often highly critical of the oppression of religious freedom that he found in Soviet society, they did find that economically, the state had been reasonably successful at creating economic equality. The trip would have a profound impact on the journalist, deepening his own already considerable mistrust of Communism and reaffirming his own conviction that the Catholic Church must work harder to counter it through implementing Catholic social doctrines.

After his return to England, he published a reflection on his journey in which he described the material conditions in Russia as "tolerable enough." But he was shocked by the overt campaign against religion of all forms. Though some churches remained open and he was able to attend Mass at a Catholic Church in Moscow, he discovered that outside the churches, no religious teaching was allowed. In fact, public schools carried on extensive propaganda campaigns to convince the young students that religion was an old-fashioned superstition. "We hold firmly and say clearly that we wage war against religion," he was told by the headmaster of one of Moscow's largest schools. On the sides of buildings he saw graffiti mocking priests and union posters condemning religious beliefs, samples of which he took home.

But, though shocked by Communist oppression of religion, he was even more shocked on his return to England by the lacklustre response to his concerns, particularly among his own English and American fellow journalists. "When I came back to London and talked about my Russian discoveries with responsible people in the journalistic world, I was again astounded to find that what I considered the worst feature in Russia was regarded by them as the best."

He saw this hostility to religion as an ominous sign of worse things to come in Europe and North America. "Some day or other the real fight in the world will not be about markets or territories, but about the fundamentals of Christian morality. I know which will be the side of Russia, and which will be the side of Poland [at that time a devoutly Catholic country – *author*]; but I am uncertain about other countries, including my own." Henceforth, he would focus more and more attention on the totalitarian and oppressive nature of Communism wherever it arose.

Unfortunately, his reports were not universally welcomed back at the *Star*, though they were popular with readers and were syndicated in Canada and the United States. Editor Harry Hindmarsh was not overly sympathetic to Somerville's concerns about religious freedom. Nor did he appreciate his correspondent's attraction to economic and social issues. He wanted lighter fare, articles on the comings and goings of royalty and the like. Hindmarsh's reaction left a bitter taste in Somerville's mouth, especially since he remained dependent on the *Star* for his income. Though he had attained a certain notoriety for his views in British intellectual circles, this had not translated into clear success for the Church on social matters, or into long-term prospects for a career in the Church.

Meanwhile, the happy couple that had wed in 1923 had become a family. A few years later, their first child, Mary, died two weeks after birth. But on April 3, 1929, a son was born, christened Peter. Family legend says Peter received his name because his parents had made a pilgrimage to Rome and prayed for a son at the tomb of St. Peter in the famous basilica named after him. Peter was followed by Stephen on April 1, 1931. Then came Anne on July 26, 1933.

The children were Somerville's great delight, but also a worry, as his career at the *Star* had abruptly ended. In June 1932, editor Hindmarsh had sent him to Wales to do a little investigation of the family tree of Hindmarsh's mother-in-law, the wife of Joseph Atkinson, owner of the *Star*. As he explained in a letter to J.H. Cranston, his old friend and fellow journalist at the Star,

> I had been in Carmarthen, Wales, for two days tracing the family of Thomas Culham and Ann Evans who were married in the eighteenth century and were ancestors of Mrs. Atkinson. I came home to find the note of dismissal. Hindmarsh said he had come to the conclusion that I was "not in sympathy with the type of journalism which the *Star* is trying to develop."

While my dismissal came as a bolt from the blue, I had long been thinking that I would be forced to quit the job. The stuff that had been wanted was such that I could not supply it and retain my self respect. Many of the subjects were largely fakes – haunted castles, family curses, clan feuds, long-lost heirs claiming fabulous fortunes, and gangsters in London. Nonetheless my sense of humour was somehow tickled at having to reply to Hindmarsh simultaneously on the pedigree of his mother-in-law and my dismissal.

Though chagrined, Somerville looked for different ways to put his journalism to work for him. He was later to feel that Hindmarsh had done him a favour – indeed, had paid him a high compliment – by telling him he wasn't cut out for bottom-line journalism. And the firing pushed him back towards what he truly loved. Over the years he had kept in touch with Archbishop McNeil back in Toronto. The archbishop had visited him in England at least once, staying at the Somervilles' small London home on Chatto Road. He proposed to McNeil a weekly column, called "London Letter," in which he would present some of the debates taking place in England. These would be published in *The Catholic Register* and syndicated to Catholic papers across Canada for $50 a week. Each article would be roughly 4,000 words and tackle subjects such as Irish nationalism, religion and various controversies. He sent a sample to the archbishop in December 1932.

But the archbishop had other plans. Rather than a London correspondent, he wanted an editor based in Toronto. McNeil, too, had been profoundly moved by *Quadragesimo Anno* and had an analysis of the Depression that closely matched Somerville's. He wanted someone of like mind within reach to help him carry on a battle in Canada against corporate greed. He also needed someone to take over from the current editor, P.J. Coleman, an

Irish journalist and poet whose poor health prevented him from carrying the heavy burden of editing a weekly paper and pushing it in the directions McNeil wanted. In August 1933, McNeil received a letter from Somerville. His persuasive abilities had proven successful once again; Somerville had accepted the archbishop's job offer, though at a salary lower than his *Toronto Star* earnings. He and his family had booked passage to Canada on the steamer *Duchess of Bedford*. It was to set sail from Liverpool on September 15. After a decade and half in England, Somerville was heading back to the new world.

Battling "isms" –
Communism, Fascism and Nazism

This September 1933 Atlantic crossing was personally momentous for Henry Somerville. For the first time, he was not travelling alone. Alongside him were his wife, Margaret, and their three young children: Peter, 4, Stephen, 2, and the infant Anne, who had been born six weeks earlier on July 26. According to her elder brother Stephen, "We crossed the Atlantic with Anne in a clothes basket because there was no place to put her." Fortunately, there was more room in Toronto. The family found immediate lodgings at the old Ford Hotel at Dundas and Yonge Streets, a spot now occupied by a commercial building. It took only a few days for Somerville to find more permanent accommodation; he rented a small house in Toronto's east end, in St. John's parish. A year later the family would buy a house in Scarborough, which was at that time a rural/urban frontier, though it is now an integral part of the city. The six-room bungalow was at 11 Thatcher Avenue, one of the more recently constructed streets. Not much more than a block away were empty farm fields that provided the young Somervilles with ample space to explore nature.

The Catholic Register office was downtown in a four-storey office building on Bond Street, sandwiched between St. Michael's Cathedral and its choir school. It was a commute via streetcar and bus that Somerville made faithfully six days a week, sometimes four times daily to accommodate evening engagements. Toronto at that time was a bustling, emerging metropolis, attracting immigrants from numerous countries in Eastern Europe to work in its many factories, railway yards and slaughterhouses. It was known as Hogtown, as it was a central processing point for pork. It was also "Toronto the Good," a city whose politics were dominated by its original Protestant Anglo-Saxon settlers; their staid Calvinist ethic gave a sombre hue to the local culture, though it couldn't hide the more colourful contributions of thousands of Irish-Catholic, Italian, Polish, Maltese, Hungarian, Lithuanian and French-Canadian residents.

Toronto in 1933 was also – like all of Canada and most of the industrialized world – in the throes of the Great Depression. The New York stock market had crashed on October 24, 1929, a day that quickly became known as Black Thursday. The crash marked the start of a drastic decline in stock values and the fortunes made on them during their heady upward climb in the previous decade. The global economy deteriorated: factories closed, currencies became devalued and millions were out of work. Canadian historian Jesuit Father Terence J. Fay describes the devastation:

> Some entrepreneurs threw themselves from office towers to their deaths, while others endured impoverishment in forced retirement at home, humbly renewing their personal and family lives. Social networks in most nations hardly existed, and the working and middle classes in most countries suffered greatly and endured the hardship in national and personal isolation…. In the 1930s, the unemployed in Montreal and Toronto walked the streets looking for work.

Canada had its own particular form of Depression hell, which it shared with the United States. Magnifying the economic downturn was a drought that, beginning in 1929, afflicted the prairies in both countries. Once known as the world's breadbasket, the prairie provinces of Alberta, Saskatchewan and Manitoba became Canada's "dust bowl" as hot, dry winds swept away fertile topsoil each summer, wiping out crops and leaving the farm families that depended on them destitute. The combined effects of the stock market crash and drought resulted in a plunge in income. Historian Ramsay Cook reports that from 1928 to 1931, annual per-person income in Canada dropped by 48 per cent, from $471 to $247.

The desperation of so many unemployed Canadians politicized them, steering their thoughts to radical solutions in the form of the newly emerging ideologies of Fascism and Communism. Though they never became as deeply entrenched as they were in Europe, these "isms" nevertheless took root in Canadian soil and were nurtured by their overseas parents. The Comintern (the organization founded after the First World War to promote Communism beyond the borders of the Soviet Union) funded and organized Communist activity in Canada, while small Fascist sects found support from home communities. Indeed, in Toronto, the Italian vice-consul made it a personal mission of his to promote a rapprochement between the Fascist government of Italy under Benito Mussolini and Italian Catholic immigrants in the city. Fearing Communism more than Fascism, Toronto's Catholic prelates found it convenient to assist Vice-Consul Giambattista Ambrosi in promoting informal co-operation with Italian pastors throughout the 1930s to preserve the culture of their congregations. It wasn't until the declaration of war turned Italy into an official enemy that the local Fascist activity came to an end.

There was more fertile soil in Canada for its own homegrown socialist-tinged politics. Various left-wing movements had existed in Canada for decades prior to the Depression, but the desperate economic conditions accelerated the growth of a labour/social movement that found successful political expression in the Co-operative Commonwealth Federation (CCF) of Canada. It sprung

from several roots: labour union activism; left-wing Prairie populism; and what became known as the "social gospel," a reading of
the teachings of Jesus Christ that emphasized social action to
achieve equality in society and fight against oppression and
poverty. Such men as J. S. Woodsworth, a Methodist minister and
Member of Parliament since 1921, and Baptist minister Tommy
Douglas imbued the movement with a moral conscience and
steered it away from violent confrontation and armed revolution.
The movement was not Communist – it competed with
Communism for the support of left-wing Canadians – but it still
caused a scare for Canadian Catholic prelates who saw it as a
stalking horse for their worst fears: atheistic socialism. In 1932,
Bishop Joseph Prud'Homme of Prince Albert and Saskatoon
issued a pastoral letter that warned against the dangers of all
forms of socialism. A year later the bishops of Quebec followed
suit with a similar condemnation. When Somerville arrived in
Canada, the ink was hardly dry on the Regina Manifesto, a document adopted in July 1933 at the first CCF convention that laid
out the party's goal to replace capitalism with "a planned and
socialized economy in which our natural resources and the principal means of production and distribution are owned and oper-
ated by the people."

Toronto had its own political complexities to deal with, and
the Toronto Catholic Church had challenges unique to its position
as the main church for so many of the immigrants who arrived on
the city's doorstep during the boom times. Canadian governments, both federal and provincial, had borrowed heavily during
the 1920s to finance the rapid growth. So had the Catholic Church
of Toronto, as it built churches to keep up with the growing rate
of immigration. From 1921 to 1931, Ontario's Catholic population grew from 577,118 to 747,000, forming 21 per cent of the
population. By comparison, Quebec had 2.4 million Catholics.

There were 36 Canadian dioceses, Toronto being the largest English-speaking one. The Toronto archdiocese included the counties of Dufferin, Lincoln, Ontario, Simcoe, Welland and York, and during the 1920s had increased from 85,000 parishioners to 128,000. In 1921, there were 159 priests in 112 parishes and missions. In 1931, there were 249 priests working in 121 parishes and missions. Religious orders supplied most of the teachers for the 59 elementary schools.

In 1933, French Canadians and major Catholic immigrant groups – Maltese, Italian, Polish, Hungarian and Lithuanian – each had at least one parish of their own. This practice tended to isolate the newcomers in ethnic ghettoes removed from the established Catholic community as well as the rest of the population. Nor did these groups have much in common with the Irish, who still dominated the Church in Toronto. An additional complication was matching the ethnicity of priests with parishes. Still, Archbishop Neil McNeil believed ethnic churches provided the most humane way to integrate the newcomers into Canadian society.

The archbishop rested his hopes for the future of the Church on promoting charity between Catholics and Protestants and providing service to the Church and the nation. Disappointed with the way Catholics lagged after other denominations in their financial contributions to the overall good of society, he constantly urged his flock to take their rightful place in serving their fellow citizens through various social projects. Catholic education was a unifying factor for the Catholic community. McNeil poured a considerable amount of money and resources into Catholic schools and was a zealous advocate for greater provincial government support for his schools. He believed these schools would be a useful bulwark against Communism, which he feared would make inroads among the immigrants from Eastern Europe, particularly the Ukrainians.

McNeil was also a strong promoter of Catholic Action. This social reform movement, encouraged in Europe by Pope Pius XI as a response to *Rerum Novarum*, was particularly geared to allow lay people to participate in the work of the Church to change society. Although it was under the direction of the bishops, lay people were the prime movers, working in co-operation with the clergy. Redemptorist Father George Daly was Toronto's biggest promoter of Catholic Action during the 1920s.

The difficulty in promoting Catholic Action in Toronto was that many of the parishes had more pressing problems to deal with – paying the mortgage, for instance. During the Depression, many parishes faced financial crises and turned regularly to their flocks to get donations through special collections. In February 1933 alone, 16 parishes defaulted on their interest payments. Meanwhile, individual Catholics had their own problems. With Jews, they were disdained by the Protestant majority, whose hiring practices were often biased. In 1928 McNeil reported to the apostolic delegate, Bishop Andrew Cassulo, that numerous major employers, including Eaton's, Bell Telephone, Loblaws and Consumers Gas, demanded to know the religious affiliation of all job applicants. Some, he said, frankly told job-seekers that only Protestants should bother applying.

This was the political landscape Somerville faced when he arrived in Toronto. The circulation of *The Catholic Register* was 19,000, making it one of the larger religious publications in Canada. Though ostensibly working side by side with editor P.J. Coleman, Somerville had de facto editorial control, as the man he had been hired to replace was too ill to compete. He immediately began to extend the subject matter of the newspaper to include social theory and economic reform. "We are searching for the

Catholic solution of the Social Question," he wrote in his "Life and Labour" column on October 26, the first since his return. "Catholic social study is a waste of time if it does not lead to Catholic social action." Like most other religious newspapers in Canada, *The Register* was fairly conservative, focusing on missionary and Church news and devotional items. Under Coleman, it hardly noted the Depression; when it did, it blamed the whole thing on the greed of wealthy individuals. When it turned its eye to the international arena, it closely adhered to a Vatican-inspired viewpoint. It praised Mussolini – no friend of the Catholic Church – for signing the Lateran Accords, an agreement with the Holy See that officially recognized a Vatican City State. It even gave Adolf Hitler credit for pulling Germany out of its economic morass and battling Bolshevism. Coleman had little stomach for the kind of social reforms Somerville envisioned. Real reform, Coleman had argued in an editorial of June 15, 1933, was "in the ideas and ideals of men," not in their institutions. Even Archbishop McNeil cautioned his flock that the Depression was the result of "individual and corporate sinful selfishness." Though more aware of institutional and political reality than most bishops, he still saw the economic hardship as a result of moral turpitude, particularly the deadly sin of greed. Somerville saw that he had his work cut out for him; indeed, he had to redo much of the work he had begun prior to the First World War.

Thus, sprinkled amid the Church news, wire service fillers, homemaking hints, weekly moral-building fiction and devotional instruction, there began to appear articles about economic theories, social reform and union politics. Right away he resurrected his "Life and Labour" column so he could have a place where he could "particularly address Catholic industrial workers and speak more personally and freely than in an editorial capacity." This column was also a guidebook to parish social study circles, in which

Somerville had never lost faith, despite their earlier failure. Somerville was quick to notice that the political atmosphere had become markedly more radical in his absence. The Communist Party was gathering support and the Co-operative Common-wealth Federation was being taken seriously as a challenge to the traditional brokerage parties. He worried that the phenomenon he had observed in Europe, of a right-wing counter-movement that toppled over into Fascism, would soon appear in Canada.

Repeating a common warning regarding the potential for an explosion of radical action on both the right and left of the polit-ical spectrum, he wrote:

> But though the ordinary working people are not thinking of revolution they are deeply discontented with the pres-ent economic system. They have no faith in it, no hope of it, no respect for it. They do not feel any loyalty, any sense of obligation, to the existing economic regime…. The Catholic working man is up against this attitude all the time. He is breathing this atmosphere of discontent, hos-tility, unbelief. It is hard for him not to be affected by it. The Catholic worker is suffering from low wages, from unemployment; he has lost his home or is in danger of losing it; he reads in the papers revelations of scandal after scandal in the economic world. Is it any wonder if he catches the revolutionary sentiment in the air, and inclines to think that there has got to be some drastic blow-up?

"Life and Labour" was the primary forum Somerville used to spread his ideas. His editorials were the second. He also wrote articles or reprinted others he had written under a pseudonym to hide the fact that *The Register* was virtually a one-man shop. He did much of the writing and editing. He also ran a considerable number of news reports and releases on the activities and views of Catholic reformers in other countries, particularly those of the National Catholic Welfare Conference in Washington, whose priest-activists were among the chief proponents of the New Deal proposed by U.S. President Franklin Roosevelt to battle the Depression. Historian Jeanne Beck notes, "Out of this mass of material, which had a tendency to be somewhat repetitious, a core program of reform can be distilled. None of the planks Somerville endorsed were original with him; he was primarily an adapter and popularizer of ideas which he believed were particularly germane to Canadian problems." Somerville did not limit himself to *The Register.* He wrote for the *Canadian Messenger of the Sacred Heart, America* (a U.S. Jesuit-run magazine) and *Commonweal* (a lay-run American magazine). Between 1936 and 1946 he also wrote four short, simple study guides for Catholic workers enrolled in social study courses. These books drew together series of articles he published in *The Catholic Register.* He also lectured to Catholic groups throughout the Archdiocese of Toronto, and sometimes beyond. Beck observes:

> Somerville was unique among the editors of church pub-
> lications in Canada during the 1930s in that he had an
> interest in and some knowledge of economics. The
> amount of space he allotted in *The Register* to this most
> secular of topics was astonishing; indeed he was one of
> the first journalists in Canada to try to familiarize his
> readers with the economic theories of John Maynard
> Keynes. His rationale for the inclusion of this material
> was that in the nineteenth century the alliance of the eco-
> nomic theories of individualism, with the philosophy of
> 'progress through industrialization,' had greatly dimin-
> ished the security and well-being of the working man;
> hence the deterioration of the worker's position had now
> become a moral issue in which the Church should

become actively involved.... Very broadly, Somerville
argued, the Depression was but the culmination of society's disregard for the teachings of the Church which
extended back to the Reformation.... His articles on economics which appeared frequently were careful, pungent
expositions of classical and modern theory in a style relatively free of jargon. In these, Somerville sometimes sac-
rificed scholarly accuracy in order to state a general principle as simply as possible. Yet they are remarkable for
their time in that any articles on economics appeared at
all in such a widely circulated church newspaper and they
do represent a unique attempt to communicate economic and social analysis to an unsophisticated audience.

Somerville attacked big business, big banks, usurious interest
rates and a fearful government that refused to attempt to put into
practice the economic theories of new thinkers such as Keynes.
He also urged Catholics to break out of their intellectual ghetto,
to look for the good in the ideas of others and work with those of
like mind, wherever they might be found. He was not in favour of
Catholic political parties, nor did he think the Church should
provide the blueprint for social reform. His range of targets was
broad. For instance, he published parts of the testimony of hearings of the Royal Commission on Price Spreads and Mass Buying
initiated in March 1934 by H.H. Stevens, federal minister of Trade
and Commerce, which looked into matters such as price-fixing.
He used these articles as an entry into an attack on corporate
power and ethics. He named names: J.S. McLean, president of
Canada Packers, was castigated for not being able to answer questions about his own company's buying and employment practices. Imperial Tobacco also faced his journalistic ire. He proposed
regulatory bodies to eliminate corporate dictatorship and ensure
corporate Canada served the interests of the nation as well as its

shareholders. He urged the establishment of a family allowance to encourage families to have babies, as the birth rate drastically declined during the Depression. He also pushed a low-cost housing program funded by Ottawa. But time and again, his columns and editorials returned to four of his favourite subjects: the moral and legal right of workers to form unions; a Catholic position on Communists in labour unions (they should be opposed by getting Catholics into leadership positions in the same unions); the working conditions unions should fight for; and the morality of strikes.

Somerville may have felt at times that he was a voice crying in the wilderness of a society that thought "social action" and "Catholic" were contradictory terms. Even his own Church was hard to convince. Yet he was not alone. In fact, he was part of a compact but highly industrious stream of Catholic endeavour and philosophy that had grown over the decades since 1891, when *Rerum Novarum* embraced modern notions of human rights and made common cause with the working classes. In England he had been in the thick of the Catholic Social Guild movement, but unfortunately it had no clear counterpart in Canada. Still, he found allies that were, if not numerous, at least devoted, learned and highly articulate.

Somerville was already very familiar with the Antigonish movement in Nova Scotia. Founded by Father James Tompkins and Father Moses Coady in the aftermath of the First World War, it attempted to combine Catholic social teachings with modern economic and political analysis in equipping Maritime farmers and fishermen to battle economic instability. St. Francis Xavier College became their base for an adult education and co-operative program for working people. By the 1930s, the movement was expanding rapidly under the direction of Coady, who was by then director of the Extension Department at St. F.X.

In Quebec, where the Catholic Church remained the dominant religious and social force in the 1930s, parishes became the springboard for the *caisse populaire*, a type of credit union that invested the funds of small-town Quebecers into regional development. This approach was meant to counteract the growth of international corporations whose profits earned in their Quebec factories were often siphoned out of the province. The *caisse populaire* was strongly supported by *l'Action sociale*, a Catholic publishing company and newspaper in Quebec City. According to Terence Fay, *l'Action sociale*

> saw itself as an instrument of education, co-ordinating diocesan activities and moulding the thought of college students and elites. With a name change in 1915 to *l'Action catholique*, the newspaper encouraged the growth of the *caisses populaires* and agricultural co-operatives. It regularly attacked the policies of the Liberal party and went after the high-profile Liberal Louis-Alexandre Taschereau.

Youth also lent their energy and passion to Catholic social action in Quebec through such movements as the Young Workers, Young Students, Young Farmers and Young Independents. On a more intellectual plane, the *Ècole sociale populaire*, founded by the Jesuits in 1910, applied itself to developing a critique of modern Quebec's society and economy, drawing on Catholic social teaching. It drew on the energy and analysis of Quebec intellectuals such as Dominican Father Georges-Henri Levesque and Jesuit Louis Chagnon.

In Toronto, Somerville found a small group of sympathetic lay people and forward-thinking clergy, including the Basilians at St. Michael's College and Redemptorist Father George Daly. But two other names cannot be overlooked. Baroness Catherine de Hueck Doherty, a Russian emigrant who had escaped Communist persecution, persuaded Archbishop McNeil to support her venture in developing services for the poor in Toronto. Her idea was similar to Dorothy Day's Catholic Worker movement in the United States; in fact, it was McNeil who introduced her to Day's work and gave her a train ticket to New York so she could meet Day in person. Upon her return, de Hueck started Friendship House, whose mission was to house and feed the hungry and homeless. Because her imperious nature often offended local pastors and administration skills were not her strong point, her local efforts lacked support. But among her friends and supporters was the editor of *The Catholic Register*; the Baroness was one of Somerville's first visitors when he arrived back in Canada. Another leading figure was Father Henry Carr, superior general of the Basilian congregation and first president of the Institute of Medieval Studies at St. Michael's College (later to become a pontifical institute). In 1931, Carr had written "Letters to Mildred: Chats on Christian Economics," in which he offered clear presentations of Catholic positions on a wide range of social questions. Carr and the Basilians created a home for wide-ranging discussion and intellectual inquiry on the intersection of faith and modern society. St. Michael's College and the Institute brought to Canada such distinguished teachers as Jacques Maritain and Etienne Gilson, allowing them to influence a generation of Canadian and American Catholics with their emphasis on Christian responsibility, individual freedom and democratic rights. Somerville was to find a ready forum for his own views in the study groups and classes at the college.

One of the more ticklish issues Somerville faced when he took over the editorship of *The Catholic Register* was the relationship between the Church and the CCF. It was a political minefield; if not handled delicately, it would put the foreign journalist at loggerheads with powerful Church prelates in his adopted home.

Several bishops, notably the French Canadians, saw nothing good in the CCF. Some members of the CCF felt the same way about the Catholic Church. Yet mutual animosity was not the whole picture. There were Catholics working on behalf of the new party and more Catholics ready to vote for an alternative to the traditional brokerage parties that had run the country since colonial times. Somerville worried that a knee-jerk condemnation by Church leaders would alienate many devout working-class Catholics.

The release of the Regina Manifesto inspired a cautious but positive response from the *Prairie Messenger*, a Catholic weekly newspaper run by the Benedictine monks of Saskatchewan. Its editorial stated: "There is plenty of evidence that the CCF is out to fight a relentless battle against the graft, corruption, the greed, the selfishness, with which the present system of capitalistic abuse is saturated. With this object of the new party we are in deep sympathy." In the newspaper's opinion, it would be wrong to "characterize the CCF organization as 'red.'" And *The Beacon*, a Catholic newspaper in Montreal, argued that the CCF program contained none of the socialism condemned by Leo XIII.

While the English newspaper editors didn't see "red," the Quebec bishops did, as did many other Catholic francophones. The Saskatchewan French-Canadian Catholic paper, *Le Patriote de l'Ouest*, denounced the manifesto as pure socialism. And *The Beacon*'s editorial ignited the wrath of Montreal Archbishop Georges Gauthier, who withdrew his official approval of the newspaper and on September 17 preached a homily warning Catholics against socialism in general and the CCF in particular.

> There are a number of persons among you...who will soon exercise their right to vote, [he declared]. I wish to warn them against those who speculate in human misery and who tend to impose measures frankly socialistic on

our young country…. Their system will only plunge us into greater depths of want…. That which saddens me above all is the thought that there are Catholics who are deluded by the promises of men who speak for the CCF.

After a meeting of the Canadian bishops in Quebec City in October, Archbishop Gauthier lobbied for a strong statement on the dangers of socialism. Archbishop McNeil, advised in advance by Somerville, suggested that more study was required before a definitive statement could be released. In the end, a statement was approved that condemned Communism, criticized capitalism for its greed and injustice, censured socialism, but did not mention the CCF. A month later, Cardinal J.-M. Villeneuve, Archbishop of Quebec City and primate of Canada, issued a pastoral statement reminding Catholics that socialism was still condemned by the pope. Somerville, who was still feeling his way in this not altogether familiar political terrain, gave the statement modest coverage in *The Register* in a story innocuously titled "Canadian bishops make declaration on social question."

Instead of tackling the bishops head on, Somerville decided there was more to gain by dissecting the CCF as he had the British Labour Party to see whether its program stood up to Catholic definitions of socialism. He used his "Life and Labour" column in November to describe the limits of Church teaching, pointing out the differences between a pastoral statement, a public speech, newspaper article and an offhand comment by a bishop. A couple of months later he said, "Many things are called socialism which are not socialism. Is that the mistake made about the CCF?" He argued that the party's stated objective – to regulate the production, distribution and exchange of goods to give human need priority over profits – was in keeping with Catholic doctrine. "As long as there is no pronouncement by ecclesiastical authority against the CCF, a Catholic is free to join that organization. The

basic declarations of the CCF," he added, "are capable of an interpretation consistent with Catholic doctrine." He suspected that if
it gained power, the CCF would become more moderate in its leg-
islative program than its rhetoric suggested. To cover his back, he
made sure his editorial line had the approval of Archbishop
McNeil.

Archbishop Gauthier in early 1934 was planning more
denunciations of the CCF, but he was criticized by Montreal
English Catholics involved in the labour movement, some of
whom were members of the CCF. Led by Joseph Wall, described
as a general organizer of the Canadian Brotherhood of Railway
Employees, the group presented a memo to the apostolic delegate,
the Vatican's representative in Canada. In the memo, they criticized the hierarchy's tendency to shriek "socialism" whenever the
CCF was mentioned without making any attempt to closely
examine its program in light of Catholic social teaching. They
also believed that the Catholic laity had the right and duty to get
involved in political or economic activity without direct ecclesiastical control. They referred to an article of Somerville's that talked
about the changing meaning of the word "socialism." It also said,
"We cannot allow ourselves to be separated from men of good
will – and common sense – by a mere word." The apostolic delegate refused to give Wall an audience and told the group to take
up their problem directly with the Archbishop of Montreal.

Their appeal went unheeded. On February 11, 1934,
Archbishop Gauthier issued a pastoral letter denouncing the CCF
and suggesting it threatened the rights of the family because it
didn't clearly describe the limitations of state power. "The least
that can be said is that it [the CCF] unquestionably offers us a
form of Socialism which does not warrant the support of
Catholics," Gauthier declared. Sharing his sentiments was Bishop

P.A. Chiasson of Chatham, New Brunswick, whose own pastoral letter at the same time opined:

> It is useless, we think, to give further proofs that the doctrine of the CCF is socialistic, or, at least, has strong tendencies towards Socialism. This is why we ask you, Dearly Beloved Brethren, to keep aloof from the movement which would fatally draw you towards the abyss of false doctrine on social life, and even, perhaps, become a menace to your Catholic faith.

Somerville continued to express an opposing view, if cautiously. He did this by quoting a recent speech in Parliament by Henri Bourassa, the Quebec nationalist and staunch Catholic, which said Canadians should not slander the new party. "Mr. Bourassa has said all I want to say about the CCF and if some of my Quebec friends object, as they have already objected, I ask them to turn their guns on the member for Labelle," Somerville wrote in his "Life and Labour" column. He found some solace in the fact that English-Canadian bishops were not so inclined to follow the lead of their Quebec peers. In Saskatchewan the hierarchy, led by Archbishop James McGuigan of Regina, issued a joint pastoral letter expressing concern that socialist ideas were being cloaked in various guises, but also criticizing "abuses of materialistic capitalism." The CCF was not singled out and nothing was condemned. For the rest of the decade, the issue remained unresolved among the Catholic hierarchy, even as the CCF gained modest political ground, winning seven ridings in the 1935 federal elections and 8.9 per cent of the popular vote. Amidst the shifts in the party's fortunes, Somerville found his attention occupied by other, more pressing matters.

On May 25, 1934, at midnight, Somerville's long-time Canadian mentor and father-substitute died of pneumonia in St. Michael's Hospital at the age of 82. Archbishop McNeil's long and

fruitful career drew accolades from all sectors of Canadian society. Even the *Toronto Star*, often not overly friendly towards
Catholics, praised the archbishop: "His Excellency did not abate
one jot of the proud claims of his Church. But he had no love for
controversy and preferred to gain support for his views by the
gentleness of his spirit rather than by the logic or even justness of
his position." During McNeil's three days of lying in state at St.
Michael's Cathedral, *The Catholic Register* reported, there was "an
unceasing procession of those who came to pay their respects" –
rich, poor, young, old, Catholic, Protestant, agnostic. Some 15,000
were outside the cathedral during the funeral Mass, which was
broadcast on radio.

Somerville was among the privileged few who were able to
spend a few moments with the archbishop as he lay in his hospital
bed in the days before his death. "Everybody is so kind," the archbishop told him as nurses served orange juice. "Everybody should
be kind to you, for you have always been so kind to everybody," the
younger man replied. "No, no," McNeil demurred.

Somerville owed much to the archbishop: his champion,
confidant, adviser and friend. Though understandably saddened
by McNeil's death, he carried on in his duties. And he carried on
with life, both professional and personal. Somerville was a chain-
smoker and obvious workaholic, working five-and-a-half days a
week, not to mention most evenings. Yet he also believed fervent-
ly in the importance of family life and being a good father.
Interestingly, for being such a reformer on political and economic matters, Somerville had little patience for social reform. He was
a staunch and loyal defender of the Catholic Church and a devout
practitioner in his personal life. If, for example, he attacked the
increase in the number of women in the labour force (which he
did, arguing that married women should stay home to preserve

jobs for men), then his family practised what he preached. His routine was a model of rectitude and respectability.

He has written next to nothing on his own family life, and even his own children knew little about his life before marriage. What they did know came largely from their mother, a warm, garrulous woman who liked to regale them with stories about relatives and ancestors. Family memories are more plentiful. By the late 1930s, the Somerville clan had two additions. Moira was born on June 20, 1935, and Janet came along July 14, 1938. The British-born siblings liked to call the youngest girls "the two Canucks." Life in Scarborough was fairly quiet, though their mother livened the house with her joy for life and music. Somerville had deliberately chosen the relative solitude of semi-rural Scarborough because he feared the influence downtown life would have on his growing children. Yet this decision meant sacrifices, not the least of which was the long commute from downtown, often late at night after regular public transit had closed down and he had to rely on inter-city buses.

Somerville was most at home with his growing collection of books or behind his typewriter. He had a quiet and sometimes stern disposition, hardened by his early years of living in poverty. Yet, as a dutiful father he built into his life regular moments of familial relaxation. Sundays, in particular, were special moments for the Somerville clan. Preparation began on Saturday, with Margaret trying to finish the housework by noon. By Saturday night, everyone had clean clothes and shined shoes for the morrow. There was also Confession, ensuring the family members were "as clean on the inside as everything was on the outside," says daughter Moira. The family went to Sunday Mass, then often spent the afternoon taking quiet walks through nearby fields or along sideroads. Sometimes they were not so quiet, culminating in singing, especially as the kids would join their father in a spontaneous, if not overly creative, ode to their home in the distance: "Oh, I can see our house, I can see our house, it's where it was before." Dinner was a highlight, topped by a dessert, such as cake, made especially for the occasion.

Family dinner was a fixture at the Somerville home, with father being present more often than not, despite the long hours he worked. Family prayer was an even more important part of life. Stephen, the second oldest child, remembers clearly the nightly prayers together:

> We had family prayers every night. Shortly before the young ones went to bed we said the Our Father, the Hail Mary, the I Believe in God and a number of short one-liners. And then three Hail Marys for special groups that we were always praying for – pastors and teachers, the Little Sisters of the Assumption that Dad had befriended in France…and one of the Hail Marys was for our relatives.

May and October were devoted to Mary, so there were rosaries every night. It wasn't always easy for a young brood to maintain the decorum needed for this heavy regimen of serious concentration on the transcendent. "Being lively kids, sometimes something funny would happen and we'd start laughing or giggling. Dad would always keep perfectly patient and calm but never joined in the laughter. So he set us a good example and he didn't berate us for falling into humour," recalls Stephen.

During this time, Somerville had few outside interests. However, he did find time to lecture, often at St. Michael's College. He was one of the first guests of a study club at the college in 1936, which was formed "to more effectively carry out a select program of Catholic Action." It followed a curriculum laid out by Somerville for study clubs in weekly columns in *The Register*.

The Early Years

Caricature of Henry Somerville, 1922, when he was 33 years old and working in England.

Bride and groom: Henry Somerville and Margaret Cooper at their wedding, 1923.

Family Life

The Somerville family in front of the veranda at 11 Thatcher Avenue, 1944. From left (rear): Stephen, Henry, Margaret, Peter; (front) Anne, Janet, Moira.

The whole Somerville clan, 1943, in their Thatcher Avenue home in Scarborough, Ontario. From left: Stephen, Anne, Margaret and Henry, Moira, Peter. Front: Janet.

Life in the 1940s

Henry and Margaret walk hand in hand in the garden at Thatcher Avenue, 1944.

Henry Somerville with his sons Stephen and Peter on a rare vacation in Lac Beauport, Quebec, in July 1946. They went there so the boys could work on their French.

Honours from the Church

Sir Henry Somerville in full regalia. He was awarded the Knight Commander of St. Gregory in 1947.

Henry Somerville, KCSG, and Charles Gilhooly, KCSG, at the official opening in 1951 of a new novitiate and mother-house for the Christian Brothers in what is now Don Mills, Ontario.

Celebrating

Henry Somerville is feted by the Holy Name Society in December 1947 on the occasion of his reception of the Knight Commander of St. Gregory. Somerville is sitting at the head table to the left of the centrepiece.

On Parade

As a papal knight, Henry Somerville was often called upon to be involved in major public liturgies, including this gathering of the Holy Name Society at Maple Leaf Stadium about 1950. Somerville, right, and Gilhooly precede Cardinal James McGuigan in the procession.

One Last Goodbye

Henry Somerville's funeral in February 1953 at Our Lady of Lourdes Church, Toronto.

Cardinal James McGuigan prays at the casket of Henry Somerville at his funeral.

Rest in Peace

Henry Somerville is saluted by Fourth Degree Knights of Columbus as he is to be lowered into his grave.

One of his more satisfying personal moments came on November 21, 1937, when he was awarded the papal medal *Pro Ecclesia et Pontifice*, in recognition of his work on behalf of the Church in both his professional and his private life. The medal, though officially from Pope Pius XI, had been the work of Archbishop James McGuigan, who moved from Regina to Toronto upon McNeil's death.

Born in Prince Edward Island, McGuigan was appointed Archbishop of Regina at the young age of 35. There he kept an open mind on prairie populism and the CCF and worked hard to help the victims of the Depression. Five years later, however, he was whisked off to Toronto to replace McNeil, where he received a warm welcome. A crowd of 17,500 people awaited the archbishop on March 20, 1934, and St. Michael's Cathedral was packed, with several thousand standing in the streets, for his first Mass in the city. In his comments to this new flock, McGuigan touched on what would become regular themes: the need to promote Catholic action and the participation of the laity in the life of the Church. Words to warm Somerville's heart, to be sure.

Though Somerville never formed the kind of intimate relationship with McGuigan that he enjoyed with McNeil, the new archbishop became a trusting superior who often turned to Somerville for advice on social questions and communications with the secular press. From time to time, Somerville drafted the archbishop's public statements. The papal medal cemented a growing warmth in their relations.

I do not feel myself at all worthy of the honour [Somerville wrote to McGuigan], yet it is most consoling and encouraging that Your Grace should take a highly favourable view of my efforts, and I am confirmed in my resolution to continue at least to try to merit commendation, and especially to serve Your Grace in the heavy tasks

that attend the administration of this great diocese. The
decoration has given exceeding happiness to those who
are dearest to me [Margaret, no doubt – *author*], and this
is not the least reason why I value it and feel gratitude to
Your Grace for its conferment.

This moment of personal satisfaction came after a year of
agonizing turmoil for Somerville, the editor of one of the leading
publications of the Catholic Church in Canada. For 1936 was one
of bloody upheaval in Spain, which was torn apart by civil war.
The Spanish Civil War pitted an alliance of traditional, nationalist, conservative and even Fascist forces led by General Francisco
Franco against a government of left-wing groups ranging from
moderately socialist to radical anarchists, which had declared
their monarchy a republic. Catholics around the world were
shocked when republican-supporting mobs killed thousands of
priests and nuns and burned hundreds of churches as an unoffi-
cial wave of anti-clericalism swept the country. They turned
against the government (except for a tiny, if intellectually illustrious, minority) and backed Franco's Falangist movement in its
efforts to topple the republicans and install its leader as head of a
dictatorship. But Catholic antipathy towards the republicans put
them against the tide of popular opinion in North America and
in large parts of Europe. In Canada, public opinion generally
favoured the government forces, seeing them as legitimately elected representatives of the Spanish people fighting against a tripar-
tite old guard of military, aristocracy and Church. Many Catholics
failed to recall how the Church in Spain, in Terence Fay's words,
"in identifying with the monarchy and the aristocracy, had failed
to serve the Spanish people and had abdicated its social mission
among the common people. In anger over their abandonment,
the people turned against the elites and against the Church."

The war was a bitter conflict, involving whole populations and fuelled by the money, weapons and even soldiers of foreign powers who used it as a laboratory to test the power of their own ideologies and military might. The war had a ripple effect throughout Europe and the Americas. Fascist Italy and Nazi Germany helped Franco, while the Soviet Union was heavily involved on the republican side. The war also stirred the passions of partisans on both sides of the ideological divide throughout Europe and North America. The tiny but passionate groups of volunteers that smuggled themselves into Spain to fight for both sides became the stuff of history books. In Canada, the volunteers for the republican side organized themselves as a private fighting force under the name of the Mackenzie-Papineau Battalion and saw heavy action, resulting in numerous casualties. They came from a tiny but intensely interested group of Canadians, some clearly Communist, others sympathetic to left-wing causes. There were more than a few Catholic working-class folk among them, though most Canadian Catholics were not that involved in inter-national affairs.

But if the majority of lay Catholics were not overly interested in Spain, those in Catholic leadership positions were. Taking their cue from the Vatican, the Canadian bishops did not mould an official position on the conflict, but this did not mean they were not sympathetic to their fellow Catholics in Spain. Pope Pius XI condemned the barbaric attacks on the Church in Spain in his encyclical *Divini Redemptoris* [On Atheistic Communism], in which he lamented that "the hatred, the barbarity, the unbridled violence with which this horrible butchery is being carried out are such as to be hardly credible in our age." The Catholic press in Canada, with a couple of notable exceptions, felt the same way.

While Catholic journalists such as C.J. Eustace wrote articles questioning Franco's leadership in the London, Ontario, *Catholic*

Record, and the Ottawa-based journal *Social Forum* did the same, most Catholic papers took up the nationalist cause and promoted Franco as someone who would protect the Catholic Church in Spain and restore order. Chief among these was *The Catholic Register.* Somerville took up the cause with a passion and anger that virtually steamed off the weekly editorial page as he railed against republican atrocities (but downplayed or excused nationalist ones). He reserved his chief ire, as well as the larger share of his column space, for the secular press that backed the republicans, particularly the *Toronto Star.* Somerville's fervour was fuelled, in part, by having seen during his 1929 visit to Russia how totalitarian Communist systems could oppress religious believers. When he saw left-leaning journalists writing what he considered propaganda from the comfort of a Western capital where support of Communism was often as much a matter of intellectual fashion as it was rooted in real commitment, he saw "red" in more ways than one.

Somerville's editorial broadsides in the nationalist cause started in the August 6, 1936, issue, a fortnight after the civil war erupted. His target was *Toronto Star* correspondent Pierre Van Paasen, whom in successive editorials over the next month Somerville accused of fabricating reports on purported nationalist atrocities from the safety of a Paris hotel. In an attempt to provoke a showdown with the *Star,* or at least prod some kind of response, he started his attack with the front-page headline "*Toronto Star* Lies About Spain" in large capital letters, the newspaper equivalent of screaming from the rooftops. His editorial inside took up four-and-a-half columns of detailed, point-by-point dissection of *Toronto Star* articles, quoting from other sources to prove his point. "The vilest kind of Red propaganda is being broadcast in Canada by the *Toronto Star,*" he said, not mincing words. Then it was on to Van Paasen: "Of all the *Star's* fabricators, the most reckless and impudent is Pierre Van Paasen…. He is not only a retailer but the originator of the most wicked kind of falsehood…. He is a poor hack giving his employers what they want. What has the *Toronto Daily Star* to say about it?"

What the *Star* had to say about it was nothing, at least not to *The Catholic Register*. Still, the *Star's* owner was stung by the accusations and investigated them, then travelled to Paris and fired his hapless correspondent.

However, this episode was a sideshow in the ideological battle waged in Canada by *The Register* and other Catholic papers. Despite the papers' best efforts, most Canadians sided with the republicans, putting the Catholic press on the defensive as it attempted to explain that the Church was not in league with Fascists, that Franco was not a Fascist and that the Church had pointed out the errors inherent in Fascist philosophy. In a January 28, 1937, editorial, Somerville observed that Catholic bishops in Belgium opposed Fascism in their own country because of its tendencies towards totalitarianism. The Church's position on forms of government, he argued, was much more nuanced than generally believed:

> She [the Church] would establish relations with the Soviet if the Soviet would allow the essential minimum of religious liberty in Russia. This would not mean she opposed Soviet economics; she scarcely approves of the economics of the capitalistic countries. The Church adapts herself, as far as possible, to the institutions of different countries; this does not mean she has any particular sympathy with those institutions.

And he would continue to point out the extent of atrocities against Spanish Catholics as new facts came to light. In February 1937, for instance, *The Register* reported that 13,000 priests and eleven bishops had been killed in the fighting and that every church in 23 dioceses had been burned. Somewhat defensively, he recognized that not all Catholics agreed with his view, notably the highly respected French philosopher Jacques Maritain, who along with a number of other Catholic intellectuals in Europe had signed a public letter urging the governments of the world to stop Franco from destroying Madrid, which he held under siege. As the nationalists were soon to overwhelm all remaining republican forces and consolidate their rule, the press battle dissipated and the world's journalists turned their attention to other issues.

While distressed by the Spanish Civil War, Somerville did not let it take over his other interests. As the world's ideological titans used the battling parties in Spain as their proxies, the struggle over the hearts and minds of working people continued else-where. Somerville turned his attention once again to pointing out the mendacity of Communists in Canada while supporting the rights of labourers in their drive for better working conditions. In March 1937, he reminded Canadians that the Church favoured unionization as a rule, "and she asserts most emphatically the right of workers to form labour associations to protect their claims to fair wages and conditions of employment." This policy was put to the test in a volatile strike in the heart of the Archdiocese of Toronto less than a month later.

On April 8, almost 4,000 workers at General Motors' (GM) huge automotive plant in Oshawa went on strike to back their demands: an eight-hour work day; better wages and working con-ditions; a system of seniority; and – the real sticking point – recognition for their union, the new United Automobile Workers. The company feared the UAW, an affiliate of the U.S. Committee for Industrial Organization (CIO), which had some Communist backing. More importantly, GM had the support of Ontario Premier Mitchell Hepburn in its strategy of stonewalling on this essential issue. Hepburn was almost apoplectic in his opposition to the notion that an American-influenced union – especially when local Communists were among their most energetic supporters – would take root in his backyard.

> The entire resources of this province will be utilized, if occasion warrant, to prevent anything in this country resembling that which is taking place across the line due to the failure of constituted authority to take adequate action [he told reporters]. We know what these agitators are up to. We are advised that they are working their way into the lumber camps, the pulp mills and our mines. Well, this has got to stop – and we are going to do it. If necessary, we'll raise an army to do it.

The Liberal premier was true to his fighting words. He ordered that all leave for Ontario Provincial Police (OPP) officers be cancelled and he asked for help from Ottawa. The federal government under William Lyon Mackenzie King sent 100 RCMP officers but balked at Hepburn's agitated request for more when there was little violence that would require police reinforcements. Stung by King's refusal, Hepburn gave the OPP authority to create their own special constables, which became known by the jeering strikers as Hepburn's Hussars and Sons of Mitch's.

This was an extremely tense situation, one that for Somerville pitted his animosity towards Communism against his reputation as a defender of workers' rights. Regarding a sitdown strike a few weeks earlier at a GM plant in Michigan, Somerville defended the workers, saying that unjust wages were a greater evil than illegal trespass, arguing that "if the law functions against trespass and no remedy is provided for the greater evil of unjust wages, the system cannot continue to command respect and loyalty." But that was a situation in another country. The Oshawa strikers were just next door, and there were local Catholics on both sides of the issue. In his first comment on the Oshawa strike in an April 15 front-page editorial, he struck a cautious but helpful note, suggesting that General Motors had a legitimate point in its fears of domination of the local union by American organizers. He suggested that the union ask its U.S. representative to "stand in the sidelines" during the negotiations. "It is simply that Canadians do not wish to appear to be signing agreements under the conditions of illegality which have governed the situation in the United States." A second editorial in the same issue reiterated Pope Pius XI's condemnation of Communism, while pointing out the Church's recognition of workers' rights.

> As far as loyal and instructed Catholics are concerned the question of the right of workers to form their own unions, not simply to accept company unions favoured by the employers, is settled beyond doubt. To hinder the exercise of a right is an act of injustice, it is sinful, and it is utterly condemned by the Catholic Church, [he declared, leaving no room for ambiguity]. As the Pope says, certain Catholic employers, by refusing to recognize the rights of working men, rights explicitly acknowledged by the Church, have done much to shake the faith of working men in the religion of Jesus Christ.

But Somerville went even further, defending the ties the UAW had with the U.S. labour movement. "It is no crime of labour unions in a country like Canada that they are international, which means that they operate both in Canada and the United States." A week later, he revisited the question, arguing that it would be wrong to exploit Catholic fears of Communism by trying to paint every trade union as a pit of Communists. Even while recognizing that the CIO had Communist support, he observed that it also had the support of Catholic workers. He repeated an oft-used refrain: the best way to banish Communist influence from labour unions was by nurturing and supporting well-educated, loyal Catholics who would vie for leadership positions in the labour movement.

The strike was peacefully settled on April 23 with the workers getting their demands, even the recognition of their union, while GM was able to push the U.S. union representatives out of the picture. "The strike at Oshawa of the 3,700 workers of General Motors has been settled exactly in the way advocated in a front-page editorial in this paper two weeks ago," Somerville boasted. And, it appears, with good reason. He was right, though it wasn't due to his own influence as much as it was that others closer to the action had the same idea.

As the 1930s progressed, tension in Europe escalated. The brewing conflict occupied an increasing amount of Somerville's attention. Hitler in Germany and Mussolini in Italy had shown that they were not content to govern their countries in peace, but had expansionist ambitions. Their totalitarian ideologies demanded that they proselytize and convert – by force if necessary – those who opposed them. Somerville foresaw the dangers of such tyranny early on; soon after he arrived in 1933 *The Register* dramatically departed from its sympathy for the Fascists of the 1920s. Mostly, this criticism took the form of reporting on opposition to the Nazis from Church hierarchy in Germany and the Vatican, or coverage of the growing hostility between Church and state in Germany, despite a concordat, or treaty, signed between the two parties as a way to ensure harmonious relations. *The Register* noted Nazi moves against Catholic political parties, schools, newspapers and fraternal societies. It recorded every German bishop who spoke out against the encroaching power of the German state. And Somerville himself issued detailed warnings about the dangers of Nazism and Fascism, particularly during the Spanish Civil War, when he was at pains to explain the Church's at times friendly outlook towards such regimes.

In August 1935, Somerville questioned whether Hitler was at war with the Church. He called Hitler a tyrant and lamented the suffering of both Catholics and Jews. Six months later, he gently criticized the Church's naïveté over its concordat with Germany.

> It was vain to think that when Hitler was destroying every other liberty, the liberty of the press, the liberty of political organization, the liberty of trade unions, that Catholic liberties would remain sacred, [he wrote on January 30, 1936]. The Socialist trade unions were suppressed first, and the Catholic unions second. The so-called "red" parties in the Reichstag were outlawed, and then the centre was terrorized into suicide. The Catholic cause was bound up with the cause of liberty and justice. Failure to perceive this may have been the capital blunder.

In April 1936 he again noted – in a bit of prescience – the suffering of the Jews, though it was in an editorial defending the Church in Austria, which had been accused of anti-Semitism. "We favour no discrimination against Jews. Neither do we favour discrimination for Jews. They have no right whatever to attribute feeling against them to 'clericals.' It is the 'clericals' who have saved Austria from the Nazis, and the Jews would expect very short shrift from the Nazis."

Pius XI gave Somerville another chance to warn of the dangers of Hitler when the pope issued his encyclical *Mit Brennender Sorge* (On the Church and the German Reich). Issued on Palm Sunday, March 14, 1937, in German, the clear denunciation of Nazi ideology was smuggled into the country and read from the pulpits. "The encyclical denounces the racial doctrines of the radical theorists," *The Register* reported. Somerville continued to clarify the Church's position on Communism and Fascism, arguing that "so far as it is necessary to protect her spiritual interests she fights both these enemies at the same time." He warned Catholics to be careful in their battle against Communism that they do not lean too far to the right, allowing their critics to identify them with Fascists.

As 1938 unfolded, Somerville became even more worried about Nazi expansion. The Anschluss, or annexation of Austria, in February was, he said, "the most profoundly disturbing event that has taken place in the world since the end of the last Great War." *The Register* reported with sadness a public statement by the Austrian bishops in support of the new regime as long as religious rights were protected, though it also pointed out that the Vatican had not been informed ahead of time of the Austrian bishops' position and roundly attacked it on Vatican Radio. In May, Somerville editorialized that anti-Semitism was "so utterly unChristian," as he defended Jews against accusations that they were behind most Marxist movements worldwide. Two months later, he returned to the subject, observing that "the fate of the Jews is more cruel than that which Catholics are forced to suffer" in the Third Reich. He urged Catholics to help persecuted Jews. "A real emergency, one of the most tragic in history, is challenging the world, especially the Christian world." Significantly, Somerville made these comments before the world was aware that Hitler was heading in the direction of the Final Solution, or extermination of the entire Jewish race.

Despite his sympathy for the Jews, Somerville cannot be judged by modern standards applied towards anti-Semitism, especially since the Second Vatican Council, when the Church began to revise its ancient hostility to the Jewish race. As a devout Catholic, he shared the certainty of the vast majority of his co-religionists of the time that the ultimate salvation for Jews would be found in conversion to Catholicism. His words would grate on modern ears: "The Jews are under a doom because they have rejected Christ and it is only by being reconciled to Him that they can save themselves. One day, by God's mercy, the Jews will come into the Church; meantime they must expiate their sin of unbelief and Catholics should regard them with the passionate spirit displayed by St. Paul."

On February 10, 1939, one of Somerville's heroes of Catholic action, Pius XI, died. In his editorial following the pope's passing, Somerville praised the pontiff's courage in withstanding totalitarianism of both left and right. "He became the world's outstanding champion of the rights of man," he wrote. The next pope, Cardinal Eugenio Pacelli, took the name Pius XII upon his election on March 2. Pacelli had been a senior Vatican insider with extensive experience in diplomacy, including having a hand in the development of the dubious concordat with Germany. Still, Somerville saw the new pope's international experience as a strength.

In the months leading up to war, Somerville began to believe that his old nemesis, Communism, was not as great a threat as Nazism. "To save a country from Nazi domination is one of the highest possible goods," he wrote in April. "Whether Nazism is in itself as bad as Communism may be arguable but there are grounds for regarding it as more dangerous to the Catholic Church than Communism could ever be." As Hitler became more belligerent in his demands on neighbouring countries, Somerville began to muse that it might take an alliance between France, Britain and Russia to defeat Germany. "Their purpose would be the defence of their own liberties, including their religious liberties, and any help that accrued to atheism in Russia would be but an indirect result," he argued, citing the theological principal of "double effect" in which an act done for a moral purpose can also have bad consequences but nevertheless may be pursued as long as the good outweighs the bad. The very next week Somerville would praise Britain's promise of a security guarantee to Poland in case of German invasion. "Britain had excellent reasons for her alliance with Poland. The Poles are magnificent fighters and are never quitters." Clearly, he underestimated the power of the Nazis.

War appeared inevitable that summer. Yet the threat of war didn't stop Somerville from taking his entire family on another Atlantic crossing. On August 12, the clan set sail on the *Empress of Britain* to visit England and celebrate the ordination into the Society of Jesus of Somerville's brother Francis. They planned to be there about a month. At dawn on September 1, Germany attacked Poland. Britain declared war on Germany two days later; Canada followed suit within a week. The Second World War had begun.

Momentous Changes

It was an idyllic visit to the homeland for the Somervilles. The relatives in Leeds were hospitable hosts and the ordination of Father Francis Somerville in August 1939, when he joined his older brother Charles in the Society of Jesus, was a great celebration. But it would soon be time to face the journey home. This one held ominous significance: Britain was at war and the security of the ship could not be guaranteed against attack from German submarines.

Henry Somerville's worry increased sixfold, as Margaret and their five young children were with him. Understandably, the Atlantic crossing was a tense time for the Somerville elders, though the children found it all rather exciting, especially the regular emergency drills, complete with lessons in using gas masks and life vests. Stephen Somerville recalls the trip: "The *Athenia* passenger liner had been sunk and my mother was scared to death. It wasn't realistic to me so I somehow took it all calmly. I think I got a bit seasick."

Back in Toronto, Canada was becoming a country at war. Recruitment of a volunteer army had begun, though there was as yet little talk of conscription. That year the always financially cautious Somerville had dug into his pocket and purchased a radio, his first and only concession to twentieth-century communications. But he made it clear to the family that this new appliance was not a toy or entertainment centre: it was a tool to keep in touch with the news of the war (and later the visit of King George VI to Canada). The daily reports became an important source of information, particularly during the Battle of Britain, when bombs were destroying British cities and the Somervilles worried about the safety of their relatives back home. Somerville would never listen to the radio shows popular at the time, though Margaret was known to listen to her favourite show, *The Happy Gang,* at lunchtime.

The Somerville family settled back into domestic life. It was an austere lifestyle, even for the times. There was only one income, that of an underpaid editor of a small Catholic weekly newspaper. And their father had always been extremely careful with money, a result of growing up poor in Leeds. The children recall a childhood that was happy, due largely to the efforts of their mother, who creatively stretched the meagre resources at hand to ensure that her children had rich, if not expensive, experiences. Human memory being what it is, the surviving children have slightly different recollections of how much money their mother had to spend weekly on groceries and household items (it ranged from $10 to $20, while daughter Moira recalls her father earning $100 a week in the later years of his life), but all remember there was little extra for many things their friends took for granted. A pair of leather shoes, bestowed on each child in the fall, had to last until summer. The girls wore standard uniforms of a tunic and blouse to school. The two boys, Stephen and Peter, began to attend St. Michael's Choir School downtown in 1939, but had to take public transit with their father to get there; the Somervilles never owned a car. They didn't own a refrigerator either, because their father thought it a luxury; after his death, the then adult children chipped in and bought one for their mother. Meals were simple, though nutritious, and varied little from day to day. "We had to eat small portions of food and dessert and meat," recalls Stephen. "We didn't go hungry but we didn't eat fancy or lavishly. There was never pop. Candies only once a week.

Dad would bring home a few candies every Friday night. They would last all weekend."

Margaret looms large in the family life at the Somerville home. She lived to be 92, outlasting her husband by 30 years. Despite often being sick throughout her life, she poured herself into creating a rich, lively environment for her husband and children. She used the fields surrounding their home to teach her children lessons about nature. Both boys became avid amateur naturalists, delighting in recognizing and naming the local birds and plants.

Having come from a family that, though working class, had attained a certain gentility in England, she introduced her children to literature and music. Margaret's talent shone particularly in music. She was a capable pianist, able to learn a melody by ear, and she insisted that all her children learn to sing, while both boys took piano lessons. That influence was powerful: all the surviving children continue to love singing and have strong voices; Stephen became a notable priest-composer and organist, playing regularly for Mass from the time he was eleven; Peter, who was also a priest, taught at St. Michael's Choir School early in his career. Family singalongs were a staple of evening entertainment at the Somerville residence as the children picked songs out of the Scottish Student's Songbook or attempted popular tunes of the time.

Their father would also join in, though he usually remained in the background. His influence over the children was apparent in the books he chose to read to them when they were young: lives of the saints; or poetry, such as G.K. Chesterton's "Ballad of the White Horse"; or Scripture passages. Though usually reserved and undemonstrative, he was known to relax after supper with the children, letting them cajole him into the traditional father role of pony on the living room rug. Moira, who believed her father had a particularly soft spot for her, would often sit on his lap after supper and mould his thin and wispy Brylcreemed hair into little tufts, sometimes tying them with ribbons. She recalls one occasion when her father, always a little absent-minded about his appearance, went with bows in hair to answer the door. Fortunately, his wife caught him on the way and saved him from an embarrassing situation.

The relationship between the parents was always one of mutual love and respect, yet it was clearly traditional. Margaret strove to please her husband, but he seemed to notice very little. He kept control of the money and told her little about how it was spent; after his death she had to be taught how to write a cheque. Money was always a worry for Somerville and he doled it out in small amounts, though from time to time he was known to indulge in spontaneous acts of generosity to others. Once, a loan or gift of $500 to a young immigrant to set up a small business raised Margaret's eyebrow, as the family could have used this significant sum at the time, but she didn't make an issue of it.

There were differences, too. Margaret was much more class conscious than her husband and sometimes winced when he used colloquial English or bits of slang that revealed his working-class roots. They disagreed on most political matters, Margaret loving the British monarchy, its aristocracy and all things reminiscent of Merry Old England, while he was a democrat. To keep the peace, they rarely talked politics, which was not uncommon for couples of the times.

Outside the domesticity on Thatcher Avenue, the world was gearing up for a long war. The leadership of the Catholic Church in Canada had not been enthusiastic about the prospects for war; their words at its outset were cautious, though patriotic. In Somerville's absence in August, a *Catholic Register* editorial sombrely urged Catholics to "stand by their country" and encouraged them to pray for peace while pointing out that Canada's place was at Britain's side. Toronto's Archbishop McGuigan issued a carefully worded statement:

> Canada will take her place, calmly and steadfastly, side by side with Great Britain, primarily to defend her own shores and our own Canadian homes. We have been forced to meet the challenge of a principle which, if it prevailed, would enslave the human soul, would destroy the freedom and dignity of the human personality and our fundamental belief in immortality and our own eternal destiny.

McGuigan clearly saw Nazism as a challenge to the beliefs of Catholics as much as a security issue. Yet he also seemed to think Canada's involvement could be restricted to its own borders, a bit of wishful thinking that was a minority view in Canada and would soon be proven wrong.

As the war progressed, Catholics, and *The Catholic Register*, warmed to the task of fighting the Nazis. Somerville had no qualms about defining the conflict in terms of atheist Nazis against Christendom: "A crusade is a war for a definitely Christian interest," he argued in an editorial in December 1939. "The triumph of Nazism in the world would be a most terrible danger for the Church." *The Register* continued to urge Catholic involvement, through either volunteering for the armed forces or buying Victory Bonds to help the government finance the war effort. On its news pages, it continuously found room for articles on Nazi atrocities, ranging from a euthanasia program against the physically and mentally disabled to the genocide of the Jews, which was by then becoming increasingly apparent to the world. In those early years of the war, before the Allies were joined by the United States and Britain was under siege, when victory seemed to be close for the Germans, Somerville urged his readers not to lose hope: "Those who spread thoughts of defeat are weakening their country. Pessimism is foolish and it is disloyal. Faith has its part in patriotism as well as religion."

As the war went on, so did life in Canada. Somerville continued to be concerned about the economic well-being of the Canadian worker, though the war had vanquished the Depression by creating hundreds of thousands of jobs, either as soldiers or as workers in the factories needed to fill the demands of war for steel, vehicles, ships, planes, munitions and supplies of all kinds. Looking ahead even then to Canadian post-war society, he turned his "Life and Labour" column into "Where Do We Go From Here," a weekly column devoted to the problems of reconstructing a peace-time economy after the war. Not all its contents were on future matters, however, and he often engaged in debate on current economic issues such as housing, interest rates and fluctuating currencies. In his editorials he turned to other social problems, raising concerns about racism against African Canadians (then known as Negroes) or defending the traditional family against the evils of easy divorce.

The year 1942 brought a dramatic change to Somerville personally, and to *The Catholic Register*. In an effort to increase awareness of the work of the Catholic Church Extension Society, a fund-raising agency that helped finance the mission activities of the Church in the far north and west of Canada, the bishops of Ontario decided to combine most of their diocesan newspapers into one. *The Register,* whose full name was *The Catholic Register and Church Extension,* had been the flagship of Ontario's Catholic newspapers and the bearer of a page each week of news about the Extension Society. By combining the circulation of *The Register* with that of five other newspapers, Extension would be able to reach far more Catholics with its plea for contributions and descriptions of the work of the Church among the Inuit and other First Nations. On February 19, the front page of *The Catholic*

Register announced the creation of *The Canadian Register,* bringing into its pages *The Register, The Canadian Freeman* (published in Kingston), the *Montreal Beacon, The Crusader* (Pembroke, Ontario), and *The Northern Catholic* (Sault Ste. Marie). It would start life with a circulation of just over 40,000.

The new weekly would be a 12-page broadsheet, printed in Kingston on a press formerly used for *The Freeman.* Somerville would be editor, but he would share that honour with Father D.A. Casey, formerly of *The Freeman.* Also on the masthead was Father S.B. Plunkett of Kingston as managing editor and Father J.G. Hanley, also of Kingston, as associate editor. Somerville, besides writing editorials, would continue to be responsible for the Toronto pages. But the other pages would be laid out in Kingston, where the editorial crew there would choose stories for the front page and elsewhere in the paper, and do all the production. On the editorial page itself, Somerville would share duties with Father Casey and Father Hanley. Readers would be able to tell who wrote which editorials by the initials at the bottom. There would also be uninitialed editorials, usually representing the common opinion of the editors.

The *Canadian Register* project had been under consideration since 1936, when the bishops of the ecclesiastical provinces of Toronto and Kingston met; a discussion was held but no further action taken. Then, in 1939, the bishops discussed the idea at more length and asked the *Canadian Freeman,* which was already publishing four diocesan weeklies under its banner, to make a proposal. The bishops considered their proposal at meetings in the fall of 1939 and again in 1940. The following year, more details were added to the proposal and it received the bishops' collective approval in the fall, with a winter kick-off planned. The bishops' hopes for the new publication were twofold: to help Extension raise more money, and to create a more efficient tool for moulding Catholic opinion in English-speaking Canada. It was hoped that more diocesan publications would come on board later; by year's end *The Prospector* newspaper of Nelson, British Columbia, had joined.

The Canadian Register was a flashier version of its predecessors. There were larger photos, and more of them. A women's page offered everything from serial novels to recipes to clothing patterns. A children's page provided lighter, wholesome fare and even comics, such as "Catholic Firsts," a Guinness Book of Records-type of comic featuring great feats by Catholics around the world; and the Smith Family, rich Americans who moved from the city to a ranch in the Rockies where character-building episodes ensued each week. Church Extension had two pages for its own news, as did the local dioceses. The front page was reserved for the larger issues of the day – international, national and provincial – though the occasional local story would make it there if it had wider significance.

The new publication was praised by Archbishop McGuigan in Toronto, who told readers that he was shocked to learn how few Catholics took a Catholic paper of any kind in their homes. He urged his own pastors to push the new paper, saying, "*The Canadian Register* should be sold at the church doors every Sunday in a stable, permanent and dignified way." Somerville's own view of this change of events is not known, though he carried on as gamely as ever, pushing sales of the paper in the news pages and even recruiting his own children to help sell subscriptions door to door in Toronto. The arrangement of shared editorials allowed him to specialize more on those issues dear to his heart, notably the war, the fight against Communism and labour issues. He also continued writing his column "Where Do We Go From Here."

One of the first major national issues *The Canadian Register* had to deal with was conscription. The draft for Canadian military forces had been highly controversial in the First World War, sparking riots in Quebec and elsewhere between forces pro and con. Canada's political leadership thus approached the topic gingerly in the Second World War, knowing how volatile public opinion was. In fact, Prime Minister William Lyon Mackenzie King had before the war vowed that he would never introduce conscription again. Yet, as the war progressed, advocates for a conscripted army became more clamorous, especially when it became clear that the major army desired by the military leadership could not be supplied by volunteers alone. In the spring of 1942, to satisfy the military's demands, King asked Canadians to vote in a non-binding plebiscite on whether to release him from his vow. The results on April 27 underscored the deep divisions in Canadian society, particularly between French-speaking and English-speaking voters. Quebec, along with a few small regions with large Eastern European populations, voted overwhelmingly against conscription, with 72.9 per cent of voters saying no. English Canada was just as strongly in favour: 82.3 per cent in Ontario; 82.4 per cent in Prince Edward Island; 70.4 per cent in Alberta, to name a few provinces. Overall, 2.95 million voted in favour of conscription versus 1.64 million against. The ensuing uproar led to the resignation of federal cabinet ministers, cries of betrayal and treason from newspaper editors and accusations of cowardice levelled against French Canadians by their English counterparts.

Somerville, though favouring conscription, sought to explain the reasoning of French Canada to his English-speaking readers. He argued repeatedly that francophone opposition to conscription could not be taken as a sign of Catholic Church opposition to war. He portrayed Quebecers in a sympathetic light, arguing that their devotion to Canada was not in question. Fortunately, as the army was not seeing much action because the Allied forces were not fighting on continental Europe in any large numbers, conscription was not immediately necessary. And to defuse the issue, King repeated his deliberately ambiguous motto that it would be "conscription if necessary, but not necessarily conscription." By this he meant he would only issue orders to conscript soldiers when it was clear that this would be necessary to secure victory. In 1942, this strategy worked and the issue died out for the time being. In 1944, when it became clear that the army was in dire need of new soldiers, King reluctantly ordered 16,000 to be called up for service, of which 12,908 went overseas. The small number required meant that the issue would not boil over and King was handily re-elected in 1945, reaping more than 50 per cent of the votes in Quebec, the highest percentage of any province.

Conscription may have been a momentary, if touchy, crisis. But other political issues remained unresolved, particularly for the Catholic Church in Canada. The Co-operative Commonwealth Federation (CCF) had slowly gained political support across Canada for its program of social welfare benefits for families and working people and its demands to create public ownership of key industries. By the 1940s, under the leadership of M.J. Coldwell, it was a serious rival to King's Liberals. A debate – quiescent since 1938 – within the Church hierarchy over whether the CCF was a socialist party of the sort condemned by the Church as atheistic had never been resolved. Yet Canadian Catholics, many of whom supported the socially progressive program of the CCF, wanted to know where the Church stood. Since the early 1930s, when several French-Canadian bishops had condemned the party, Somerville had tried to persuade the hierarchy that the CCF's version of socialism was moderate, peaceful and wholly democratic. In fact, he argued, there was little within the party that was not perfectly compatible with Catholic social teachings. By 1942, the time was ripe to settle the issue once and for all.

Besides using *The Register* as a pulpit for his views, Somerville also worked behind the scenes, advising friendly bishops, including his own archbishop, on ways to see parallels between the CCF and Church teachings. He found an ally in Murray Ballantyne, former editor of *The Beacon* and editor of the Montreal edition of *The Canadian Register*. Nine years younger than Somerville, and the son of Senator Charles Ballantyne, a prominent Conservative and federal cabinet minister (1917–1921 under Prime Minister Robert Borden), the young Ballantyne had been a student at McGill University in the 1930s and was influenced by left-thinking intellectuals Eugene Forsey and Frank Scott, two CCF stalwarts. He converted to Catholicism in 1933 and rejoiced in the CCF as a political channel for turning the Church's social encyclicals into action, seeing the party as the rough equivalent of the British Labour Party. Ballantyne had hoped to be a bridge between the Catholic community and CCF intellectuals, but he found himself hamstrung by bishops who were highly suspicious of the party and kept him on a short leash. Years earlier, *The Beacon* had drawn the wrath of Montreal Archbishop Georges Gauthier when it mildly suggested that the Regina Manifesto contained none of the socialism condemned by the Church.

In 1940, after the death of Archbishop Gauthier and his replacement by the more open-minded Joseph Charbonneau, Ballantyne saw hope for a reappraisal by the Church. He immediately began to impress upon the new archbishop the urgent need to repair relations between the Church and the CCF. He argued that the defeat of Conservative leader Arthur Meighen by CCF candidate Joe Noseworthy in a recent by-election in Toronto was a sign that the CCF was poised to make major political gains and that it would hurt the Church if it was seen to be against such a legitimate and widely accepted political force. Charbonneau liked what Ballantyne had to say and made him his adviser on social doctrine. Meanwhile, Somerville had been enlisting the support of Calgary Bishop Francis Carroll, a transplant from Toronto who invited the editor to his diocese to give four lectures. Once he was on-site, Somerville was able to persuade the bishop that a Catholic could belong to the CCF without fear of sinning. What's more, Carroll agreed to work on persuading other bishops to make the CCF a discussion item for the 1943 plenary meeting of all the Catholic bishops of Canada, slated for mid-October in Quebec City.

Back in Montreal, Ballantyne set up a meeting for Archbishop Charbonneau with CCF leader Coldwell. The meeting took place without publicity in September 1943 at Ballantyne's house. Professor Frank Scott was also there. Ballantyne later wrote that the three men "spent several hours in amicable discussion…. On both sides the talk was frank and friendly. No major point of disagreement was found." The meeting proved decisive. Archbishop Charbonneau agreed to join Archbishop McGuigan and other bishops to press for clarification of the Church's stance. At the October plenary the bishops agreed that the Church should be "indifferent" regarding the CCF and issue a statement to this effect. It would include three points: a general appeal to promote social reforms; special mention of the social action projects instituted by St. Francis Xavier University in Antigonish, and the *Semaines sociales du Canada* in Quebec; and, most significantly, the fact that Catholics would be free to support any political party upholding basic Christian traditions in Canada and favouring needed social and economic reforms. Though the CCF was not mentioned by name, in effect, the Church was saying it was not a sin to support this "socialist" party.

Somerville played an important role in disseminating this news and putting the proper spin on it for public consumption. He and Ballantyne persuaded the bishops to let them publish the statement in *The Canadian Register* and *L'Action Catholique* accompanied by a Somerville editorial that had been pre-approved by McGuigan. In his editorial, he would not hesitate to name the CCF; by doing so, he rather than the bishops would take responsibility for any backlash from more conservative-minded Catholics. At the same time, no initials would accompany the editorial so that it would appear to have the endorsement of the Church hierarchy. In a letter to Ballantyne, Somerville spelled out what needed to be done:

> The Archbishop…is quite willing to let us have the scoop for the Catholic Press. Will you please be responsible for giving the release to the CP [Canadian Press] and the B.U.P. [British United Press] informing me of whether the release is for morning or afternoon papers first. I will advise the CP here because it is the head office and the assistant manager, Gillis Purcell, is a Catholic, but I will tell him the actual release is being made by you in Montreal.

In the end, besides the two Catholic papers, the statement was also released in *Le Devoir* in Montreal, all on October 20. Somerville's editorial was quoted extensively in the secular press, and printed completely in the *Montreal Gazette* and the *Montreal Star*. Both papers noted that it represented an official interpretation.

Though Somerville and Ballantyne were exuberant about their success, not all their associates were quite so impressed. *The Catholic Record* (London, Ontario), the *Northwest Review* (Winnipeg) and *L'Action Catholique* didn't run the Somerville editorial and later groused that the CCF still had to prove it was above suspicion. *Saturday Night* magazine published an article by a P.J. Mulrooney repudiating the editorial. *Relations*, the Jesuit French-language publication in Montreal, suggested the declaration was rather meaningless. Several prominent Catholics complained about the Church's new position and Somerville's interpretation. One, Senator J.J. Bench, even complained to the prime minister, to no avail. E.L. Dubois, president of Hamilton Motor Products in Hamilton, Ontario, complained to Archbishop McGuigan that Somerville's views did not represent those of many Catholics. "I feel very definitely," he wrote, "and I know that I am not alone in this thought (including some parish priests here in Hamilton), that Mr. Somerville is taking just a little too much for granted in using *The Canadian Register* – the recognized Catholic newspaper of this whole section of Canada – to interpret the Bishops' report." Dubois said one priest had told him he had received so many complaints he was reducing by half the number of *Registers* he sold at the back of the church. Conservative backer and Toronto lawyer Charles McCrea, K.C., also disagreed with Somerville, writing to tell McGuigan that others couldn't believe that Somerville's view on what the bishops had said was correct. "I respectfully submit the air should be cleared…. It can, therefore, be seen that *The Canadian Register*'s view is, so far, the view of only one publication. There is no proof that it is the Catholic bishops' view."

McGuigan, for his part, defended his editor, telling McCrea that "there is no doubt whatsoever but that the Bishops had the CCF in mind when they made the statement…. I could never see anything particularly wrong with the editorial in *The Canadian Register* [perhaps because he vetted it beforehand – *author*] on the Bishops' statement. If Catholics cannot vote CCF, the Church has a duty to advise them to this effect." Despite the criticism, Somerville was pleased overall with the result of his work. "For my part I am entirely satisfied with what the declaration has done," he wrote to Ballantyne later. "It has given the CCF all the clearance it could fairly ask for and it has given all the necessary guidance to Catholic consciences." The episode resolved the issue as Somerville had hoped; his work of more than a decade was done. According to historian Jeanne Beck, it represented a culmination of his struggle since his early days in Leeds to get Church leaders to recognize that left-wing political parties could be legitimate avenues for promoting the social doctrine of the Church. Whether the Church's new friendliness helped the CCF is another question. In the 1945 federal election, the party reaped only 14.7 per cent of the vote, and 28 seats; King had been astute stealing enough of the CCF program to satisfy voters that his Liberals were also socially progressive – and not tainted by socialism.

By 1944, it was becoming apparent that the Allies would win the war. Looking ahead, Somerville could see that the returning soldiers would create a booming demand for housing, which meant rising prices. While he editorialized on the need for a housing program for all, housing was also a significant personal issue. His own children were growing up and the little house out in Scarborough no longer suited their needs. The two boys were involved ever more deeply at the Choir School and their work was suffering because of the long commute. Somerville found the travel draining. Taking advantage of the abundant supply of cheap housing during the war, he purchased a more suitable home in downtown Toronto. The Somervilles moved into it on June 7, 1944, the day after D-Day, when the Allied forces invaded Normandy and began the final push to defeat the Nazis.

The new home was at 1 Cawthra Square, a tiny enclave near Jarvis and Wellesley Streets, and was within walking distance of

The Register office and the Choir School (which were next-door
neighbours on Bond Street); St. Joseph's College School, which
the three girls would attend; and Our Lady of Lourdes Church.
When the house had been built, the neighbourhood was home to
some well-heeled Torontonians. Along nearby Jarvis Street were
large, Edwardian mansions equipped with servants' quarters.
Even the Somerville home contained features of that time, including speaking tubes to issue orders to servants in other rooms. By
1944, however, few families could afford the servants to keep up
such large homes and many had been converted into rooming
houses. Though an old brick semi-detached house, it was a huge
step up in size and quality. Moira remembers it well:

> It was a wonderful house, just wonderful. Three storeys
> high, built of brick. And it had a very beautiful stone
> foundation. There was a stone porch with a rounded
> archway. It was an old house. It had three staircases, a
> front staircase and a back staircase. One staircase went up
> to the third floor only…. There was a living room and a
> passageway around, and then the dining room and there
> was a narrow passageway along behind the dining room.
> There was a big kitchen. The house was heated with an oil
> furnace but the kitchen had a Quebec heater. We kept
> coal downstairs underneath the cellar stairs so we had a
> coal fire in the kitchen…. On the second floor at the front
> there was a master bedroom, which was over the living
> room. It had a beautiful hardwood floor. There were two
> other big bedrooms on that floor…. Upstairs there were
> three more bedrooms. The boys' bedroom was right
> across the front of the house.

The master bedroom became Somerville's study and was
soon furnished with his wooden desk, a manual typewriter and
numerous shelves that were filled with books. It also had its own

fireplace. The new location allowed a more manageable lifestyle for Somerville. He now attended morning Mass daily at Our Lady of Lourdes, coming home in time to make breakfast for his wife before heading off to work. He returned home for dinner almost every night at 5:30 p.m. He would often go back to the office after supper to do some writing, though he would usually return in time to pop in on his youngest daughter, Janet, before she dropped off to sleep. "My mother would say, 'Now, Harry, don't awaken her, don't disturb her,'" Janet recalls. "But he would always come into my room and just stand there for quite a while, just looking at me and smoking a cigarette. I remember seeing the glow of it in the dark. If I felt like talking or engaging him, I would just say something."

The new home also afforded better opportunities for enter-taining. Thatcher Avenue had been too far out of town for dinner guests, but 1 Cawthra Square saw a number of them, including, on at least one occasion, a young Paul Martin Sr., a rising star in the Liberal party whose speeches on the need to build Canada's social safety net sometimes found their way into print in *The Canadian Register*. Martin was to go on to become a senior play-er in federal Liberal cabinets in the 1950s, '60s, and '70s, while his son, Paul Jr., became Canada's finance minister from 1993 to 2002, and the leading contender to replace Prime Minister Jean Chrétien.

Living on Cawthra Square was almost a short-lived experi-ence, however. A year after moving in, Somerville found himself enticed by a new job offer. Halifax Archbishop John McNally wrote to him in August, asking that he seriously consider coming to Nova Scotia to start a new Catholic newspaper. The invitation had been issued during a conversation at a chance meeting between the two men in Peterborough, but now McNally was ready to move on it. "If you still feel disposed to make a trial of helping us in that work, may I suggest to you to make a trip down to this city and look over the possibility of launching the enterprise at as early a date as can be arranged," he wrote. There is no record of Somerville's reply, but evidently word of the invitation got out because it wasn't long before Kingston Archbishop J.A. O'Sullivan, who was on the executive board of bishops that oversaw *The Register*, was urging Archbishop McGuigan to persuade Somerville to stay in Toronto. "Henry is THE *Register*, even if he feels we have not appreciated him enough," O'Sullivan wrote to McGuigan in October. "Take him away, and it would lose whatever little appeal it has for most readers." Perhaps McGuigan took his fellow bishop's advice. Somerville did stay in Toronto, ensuring that *The Register* retained its best-known asset.

Meanwhile, his journalism continued to focus on social issues. In 1945, his old friends at St. Michael's College enlisted his help once again in providing education on the Church's social teachings for working people. A non-credit course using his books of social studies was designed and night classes ensued. Basilian Father W. Dwyer directed the program and Somerville made guest appearances from time to time. Post-war reconstruction was beginning; the troops were returning home and Somerville eagerly engaged in discussions of myriad issues surrounding their presence, including jobs, education and housing. He was pleased to see that the Liberal government also took these issues seriously. A Veterans Affairs Department had been created in 1944 and a massive and generous program was developed to ensure the veterans had a good start on their lives back in Canada. This included cash bonuses that averaged $488 per veteran, plus financial help buying farmland, obtaining a university education or setting up a small business. There were generous pensions for widows and dependents, and rehabilitation for those disabled by the war. Somerville saw much good in this program, though he continued to call for federal intervention on interest rates and other macro-economic policies.

In 1946, the war was finally in the past and reconstruction was well underway. The United Nations had been created to deal with international disagreements. The cloud of Communist expansion in Eastern Europe was beginning to worry those who were knowledgeable about international politics, but the true extent of Soviet plans was not yet revealed. And Somerville found himself on an adventure he would not have considered possible. It had nothing to do with politics or social programs or economics or even journalism. He was going to cross the Atlantic once again – this time to meet Pope Pius XII.

Rome and Home

For once in his life, Henry Somerville was able to step out of his usual dignified reserve and reveal his emotions. Travelling to Rome and meeting the pope drew out of him childlike joy and gratitude, a startling demeanour in a man so routinely businesslike and cerebral. And, again in a highly unusual move for him, he shared his joy with the whole world through the columns of *The Canadian Register*.

The occasion was a consistory, or meeting of the College of Cardinals with the pope, at which Pius XII appointed more than a dozen new cardinals from around the world. It was a historic event in that Pius XII had begun a series of reforms to the College that saw its membership expand from the usual coterie of loyal Italian prelates to include a broader range of bishops from around the world, thus beginning to break the Italian stranglehold on the Vatican Curia. Among those new cardinals was Archbishop James McGuigan of Toronto, the first English-speaking Catholic bishop in Canada to be so honoured. The archbishop decided to share the momentous occasion with three close advisers: Monsignor John Harris, his chancellor; a Father Allen; and one Catholic journalist, chosen because of his status as confidant of the archbishop, to be sure, but also to record the event for Catholics back home. This Somerville did, in copious detail, related in hundreds of column inches to *Register* readers in February and March 1946, and then collected, along with photographs, in a hard-bound book called *Rome and Home* that was published the following year.

Somerville's record of the trip, which took more than three weeks, begins with the arrival on January 22 of the small group's cruise ship, *Gripsholm*, in Naples, Italy – his eighth Atlantic cross-ing. During the crossing, Archbishop McGuigan had celebrated Mass early on each Sunday morning and preached at other Masses. The dispatch Somerville sent back to *The Register* gave a minutely detailed account of the passage, including summaries of the archbishop's homilies, passenger lists and a little verse from Robert Browning. His vivid descriptive style would characterize the reportage of this journey and was geared to help readers "see" what was going on in the pre-television age, when the only images they had were either photographed in black-and-white or drawn with words.

At Naples, they were pleasantly surprised by representatives of the British Embassy to Italy and its Legation to the Holy See, who had come to greet them and drive the group to Rome. The Canadians had been prepared to take a train – only a 160-km trip but one that, due to war damage, took over ten hours. They were grateful for the alternative. Over the next month, they would have plenty of contact with the British diplomats; owing to the absence of official relations between Canada and the Holy See, the British had taken it upon themselves to treat the Canadians as loyal and important subjects of the British Empire (which they were, in these days before the creation of the Commonwealth). The British did their utmost to make the visitors welcome, hosting receptions and luncheons for them and providing a car for the archbishop while he was in Rome.

The time in Rome was a whirlwind of official receptions, informal meals, many Masses and major public events. The Canadians stayed at the convent of the Sisters of the Precious Blood in a section of Rome that stands on the Janiculum, one of Rome's seven hills. The Sisters were from Canada and their convent was founded from the diocese of St. Hyacinth, Quebec, so they knew how to make their visitors feel at home. From this

base, the Canadians set forth on their daily rounds of visits, official and otherwise. A highlight for Somerville was a chance to
give a speech on Vatican Radio, a short-wave broadcaster whose
station was in the papal gardens behind St. Peter's Basilica.
Somerville gave a short lecture on the history of the Church in
Canada, introductory high-school textbook stuff for most
Canadians, but news to many of his listeners. He also took great
joy in a dinner hosted by T.J. Kiernan, the Irish Minister to the
Holy See, who was an old friend of Somerville's from his days as
a *Toronto Star* journalist. There was plenty of Irish humour and
good food, though, Somerville noted, no Irish whiskey. There
were also moving eucharistic celebrations at such historic sites as
the tomb of St. Peter in the basilica that bears his name, and at the
tomb of St. Paul at another of Rome's four major basilicas, St.
Paul Outside the Walls. There was as well a special Mass at Santa
Maria del Popolo, one of Rome's most popular monuments, an
ornate medieval church whose construction on the site of
Emperor Nero's tomb had begun in 1099. It had been given to
the Toronto archbishop as his titular church (titular churches
were bestowed on all cardinals in a tradition dating back to the
early days of the Church when cardinals were local pastors).
Everywhere they went, the Canadians found their egos continually fattened with praise from those they met, including many
visitors from other countries, all of whom seemed to have a generally high opinion of Canada.

Before the consistory itself came an event about which
Somerville was positively rapturous: a private audience with Pius
XII. The archbishop had requested one immediately on his arrival
in Rome, but nothing was certain about when, or even if, it would
be granted. Moreover, there was no guarantee that the archbishop
would be allowed to bring his friends. There was a fair amount of
suspense involved in waiting each day to find out whether that

would be *the* day. A week after their arrival, the invitation finally came: the audience was to take place at 10:15 the following morning. It named only the archbishop, but he insisted that the other Canadians come along and he would ask permission to present them to the pope. Before Somerville went to bed that night, he anxiously went over his wardrobe. He had packed formal evening wear for just such an occasion and he checked everything over – tail coat, white vest, boiled shirt, starched collar and white tie – to ensure all was in order. It was.

As they had hoped, all three of the archbishop's associates were allowed to be presented to the pope after the archbishop had a short private session. Monsignor Harris, Father Allen and Somerville went in together to see the pope in his private office, having been instructed beforehand about proper etiquette. They were clearly overwhelmed by the occasion. They had nervously asked the pope's chamberlain whether it was necessary to make three genuflections, as they had heard. "You make them if it is possible," shrugged the chamberlain. "If there is not time you do not make them." Somerville was relieved by the suggestion of informality; nevertheless, all three men were careful to make their three genuflections. "We were just warmed by the sunshine of the Pope's smile, and the encouraging look in his large, kind eyes and his gentle but hearty words of welcome made us feel of him as our affectionate Father," he wrote, adding, "Monsignor Harris kissed the Pope's ring at least six times."

Monsignor Harris was not the only one so moved. When Somerville was introduced by the archbishop, he was in such awe he forgot to get up from his kneeling position at the pope's feet. When the pope asked him a polite question about his children, the hard-nosed journalist found himself babbling like an excited child:

My heart was so elated and opened by his fatherly manner that I forgot all reserve and spoke with a freedom which no other human being ever drew from me. The Holy Father listened just like a father to a candid child and answered with words of interest and encouragement. He noticed my medal, that it was the Cross Pro Ecclesia, and I answered that it was given to me by Pope Pius XI. The Holy Father then gave me a rosary and a blessing, a blessing for all my dear ones, as he had done to Monsignor Harris and Fr. Allen. It was really time for me to stop but in my joy and confidence I spoke again and said how much benefit and guidance I derived from his Holiness' encyclicals and discourses on social and international questions.

The trip to Rome would end with another private visit with Pius XII, at which the pontiff would give Somerville six more rosaries so that his wife and each child would have one. Once again, the journalist laid aside all professional objectivity in his response:

This little incident of the rosaries can be related in illustration of the Holy Father's kindness which, according to all I have heard, is shown to everyone he receives in audience. I cannot find words to describe the warmth of the feeling which he displays, and which he evokes in others, for any words which I could use would seem to intrude upon what is most intimate, delicate and sacred, but I know that those who have had the inestimable privilege of such close personal contact with the Holy Father will treasure it forever in their hearts.

After such personally moving experiences, the actual public consistory was almost anti-climatic. However, Somerville portrayed well the pre-Vatican II pomp of a Church triumphant, describing the expectant, shoving crowds in St. Peter's Basilica, the ancient grandeur of this massive edifice, and the imposing presence of the cardinals and the pope themselves, clad in their richest, most colourful vestments. The pope rode in on his *sedia gestatoria*, a throne carried by special servants, and the cardinals processed in wearing their *cappa magna*, long trains trailing on the ground. Each new cardinal received his red hat, marking his new exalted rank as a prince of the Church. It was Vatican theatre at its best.

Before heading home, the Canadians made a side trip to England and Ireland on a Royal Canadian Air Force airplane. There they were feted by the new Cardinal Griffin, Archbishop of Westminster, along with Cardinal Gilroy of Sydney, Australia, who were among the trio of British Empire prelates made cardinal at the consistory. McGuigan and the other two cardinals had a personal audience with King George VI, while the entire Canadian party was flown to Dublin to be hosted by President Sean O'Kelly and greeted by the famous Prime Minister Eamon de Valera.

If their reception in Rome and Great Britain and Ireland was heart-warming, it paled compared to the welcome the group received back in Toronto. It seemed that the entire population of the city had come out to greet their first Roman Catholic cardinal. They arrived on March 27 from the east by rail, stopping first in Oshawa, the easternmost community in the archdiocese. Cardinal McGuigan was cheered by a crowd of schoolchildren waving Union Jacks and papal flags, and greeted by municipal officials. The next stop was Union Station in Toronto at 1:30 p.m. Dense crowds filled all the streets around the station and a line of limousines waited to whisk the cardinal and his entourage away. It was more of a crawl than a whisk, however, as the cars paraded through the downtown behind high school marching bands. At

City Hall McGuigan was greeted by the mayor as well as leaders of other churches. Then it was off to the Ontario Legislature, where the cardinal was introduced to the Members of Provincial Parliament by Premier George Drew and allowed to address the legislators. Finally, he was driven to his home, Wellesley Palace, where he was greeted by Archbishop Ildebrando Antoniutti, the apostolic delegate from the Vatican to Canada.

But the day was far from over. That evening, the cardinal presided at a Eucharist at St. Michael's Cathedral, attended by 40 other bishops. The crowd for the Mass overflowed onto the streets outside and loudspeakers were set up so the people who couldn't get into the cathedral could at least hear what was being said. A few days later, on March 31, the cardinal was greeted by more than 17,000 Torontonians in a reception at Maple Leaf Gardens, where he gave a speech and basked in the goodwill of the crowd. Through it all, Somerville was there, recording the proceedings for posterity and *The Canadian Register*.

It would be reasonable to say the trip to Rome was the highlight of Somerville's long career. Yet it was not the end of the excitement, or the honours. On November 29, 1947, *The Canadian Register* jubilantly announced that its long-time editor was now Sir Henry Somerville, KCSG. The honorific and the initials signified that once again Somerville had been honoured by the pope, this time with a papal knighthood. The Knight Commander of St. Gregory, which celebrated a lifetime of high achievement on behalf of the Catholic Church, was one of the highest honours the pope could bestow upon a lay person. It allowed the "knight" to be called "Sir," as could a knight created by any secular monarch. It also came with a resplendent uniform and sword, which Somerville wore proudly at public occasions in the archdiocese, often marching stiffly in procession before the archbishop.

Somerville's achievement was recognized by his fellow members of the Holy Name Society, the lay organization he had joined in the mid-1940s. At a dinner on December 15 that was attended by the cardinal, Somerville was feted and invited to make a speech, which he did gladly:

> These are among the highest honours, the proudest privileges, that can be enjoyed by any human being, but I honestly say that I value them less for themselves than as marks of the confidence and affection of one whom I admire in a way that no words can express. It would be impertinent for me to praise our Cardinal Archbishop here before this company, and I shall not do it. I only thank him, for my admiration is equalled by one thing: my gratitude.

Even when the spotlight was shone on him, Somerville managed to turn it towards someone he thought deserved it more.

But the late 1940s were not all excitement and adulation. There was still *The Canadian Register* to edit, editorials to write and subscriptions to solicit. To his discomfiture, Somerville found himself witnessing, and indeed presiding over, the apparent death of one of the premier institutions in the Catholic press in Canada. There were signs of dramatic changes in store, but Somerville either couldn't see them or was powerless to stop the current of events.

This episode began in Montreal in 1948, with a charming trilingual journalist with formidable international experience and ambitious plans to create a Catholic publication in Canada to rival England's *The Tablet* or *America* in the United States for influence on public policy. Robert W. Keyserlingk, Canadian manager of the British United Press (BUP), was able to persuade several key prelates in the Church, including Montreal's

Archbishop Charbonneau, that his plan to create *The Ensign*, a weekly tabloid newspaper, was both feasible and necessary if the Church was to retain its ability to help shape society according to God's kingdom. Keyserlingk cut an impressive figure. Born in either St. Petersburg, Russia, or Lithuania (there were conflicting reports on this) to a commander in the Russian Imperial Navy, he had fled Russia with his parents in the 1917 Bolshevik Revolution. Eventually the family found their way to Vancouver, where he studied economics and history at the University of British Columbia. He had spent years as a foreign correspondent for BUP before settling in Montreal in 1938. In 1946, he converted to Catholicism and, from that time, had a passion for putting his journalistic skills to work on behalf of the Church.

The first the public knew of Keyserlingk's ambition was in June 1948, when *The Canadian Register* published an article announcing the creation of *The Ensign*, to be published by a new firm, Campion Press Ltd. It would, the article said, draw on existing news services and a network of correspondents. "What we envisaged was a strong, vocal, interesting, aggressive and virile lay Catholic national journal, read from coast to coast, not only by Catholics, but by all those, from prime minister to editor and reporter, who must keep posted on what the Catholic world is interested in, what it is doing, what it is thinking, and what it cannot tolerate," he told the newspaper. Keyserlingk didn't tell the public his plan was not simply to create a new publication from scratch. He wanted it to replace existing diocesan newspapers and, using economies of scale, publish one large, powerful periodical with a circulation of at least 100,000.

Keyserlingk had presented his proposal to Archbishop Charbonneau in early 1948. Soon afterwards, with Charbonneau's help, Keyserlingk was able to pitch his idea to Cardinal McGuigan in Toronto. But the Toronto archbishop had his doubts. In March he wrote to Keyserlingk, saying he would hang on to his *Canadian Register*. He feared losing a place for Church Extension Society news, which, since it officially owned *The Canadian Register*, had an assured outlet. The cardinal had established himself as the doubting Thomas in the scheme, a role he would play to the end. Keyserlingk was not to be put off, however, and he went ahead by obtaining Church money to purchase the Montreal edition of *The Canadian Register*, the *Catholic Record* of London and the *Northwest Review* of Winnipeg, and cementing plans to begin publication of *The Ensign* on October 30. Seeing the momentum building, the Ontario bishops decided to revisit the issue and persuaded McGuigan to climb on board. All editions of *The Register* would now be part of *The Ensign*, including the all-important Toronto edition, based as it was in Canada's advertising capital and its largest English-speaking diocese.

On October 9, the front page headline on *The Canadian Register* shouted "*Canadian Register* in Merger with *Ensign*." It announced to readers what those working inside the Catholic press would already have known. The paper would be printed in Kingston but have its head office in Montreal. Somerville (now referred to as "Sir Somerville") would be editor of its Toronto operations. In the following week's *Canadian Register*, the shape of the staff of the new publication became clearer. It could not have been anything but disquieting for Somerville. Keyserlingk would be publisher, but Somerville's old ally Murray Ballantyne would be editor-in-chief. Managing editor was George V. Fraser of the BUP Toronto office. Somerville was fourth on the masthead, along with several other diocesan editors who were absorbed into the new publication.

As promised, *The Ensign* began publication on October 30 and *The Canadian Register* disappeared. There were eight pages of Quebec news and another eight of Ontario news, along with

Church Extension news. But it wasn't a smooth launch, and the troubles didn't abate. Cardinal McGuigan did not like what he saw, being disappointed with what he believed was too much international news, to the detriment of Canadian and local articles. He also found off-putting the heavy emphasis on "Reds" and the secular tone. On November 11, he complained to Archbishop Alexandre Vachon of Ottawa about *The Ensign*, lamenting that the bishops had no real direction over the publication and wondering whether Keyserlingk would be willing to use *The Ensign* when the Church found itself in battles on such issues as Catholic separate schools. The mix of stories improved with subsequent issues, but the cardinal refused to be mollified. It didn't help that Keyserlingk seemed to have a fixation on Communism that went far beyond even Somerville's own concern. At other times he showed odd news judgment, running articles about obscure matters in Eastern Europe that were unlikely to interest Canadian readers.

There is no public record of what Somerville thought about the new publication. He never uttered a negative word for the record. However, his family knew he was unhappy with the new arrangement. The children remember him grumbling at home about *The Ensign's* quality and their mother expressing disdain for the new paper, which was likely a reflection of her husband's views. She also harboured great suspicion of Keyserlingk, seeing his charm as a cover for a manipulative mind. Their father was, despite his humble demeanour, a proud man, sure of his craft and hard-earned expertise. "Maybe Mum said it," recalled daughter Moira. "But I certainly perceived that Dad was the kind of man who couldn't have anybody less than the archbishop as his boss."

When the opportunity arose, *The Ensign's* opponents moved quickly to take advantage. There were technical problems on two fronts. *The Register's* books were such a mess that the legal merger between it and *The Ensign* had not been completed even as late as January 1949. Moreover, problems at the press in Kingston forced Keyserlingk to move the printing job, first to the *Kingston Whig Standard* and then to an Oblate press in Ottawa. This latter switch was to take place on February 28. But when the move was completed, a number of significant players were missing from *The Ensign* team. With the Kingston plant now free, *The Register* was resurrected with the support of the dioceses of Toronto, Kingston, Hamilton and London. And *The Ensign* was banned from Toronto churches.

Somerville was returned to his old position and *The Canadian Register*, after an absence of only four months, was alive once more. Keyserlingk tried desperately to effect a reconciliation between himself and the cardinal, but with no success. *The Ensign* struggled along until 1956, when debts and declining circulation finally killed it. Keyserlingk was to blame Somerville for souring the cardinal on *The Ensign*, but it was clear from the beginning that the cardinal was not a solid backer and missed having his own publication, under his control, to promote local projects such as school and church building. Keyserlingk didn't show that he understood his readership as well as he should have. In the end, without Toronto support, *The Ensign* didn't stand a chance. It was a disappointing end for a project that held much promise as a lay-led, independent Catholic publication that would break out of the mould of the traditional diocesan press. Even today there are living memories of the enthusiasm in which *The Ensign* was greeted in some Catholic circles, and the bitterness at its demise.

Somerville could now return to doing what he loved best: writing and promoting Catholic social doctrine. In January 1950, he was involved once again in a plan to develop Catholic leaders who understood their Church's teachings and their society's economic and political structure. The Catholic Labour School began as a response to requests from Catholic members of labour unions. Somerville helped to get two schools going, one in each end of Toronto. Jesuit Father C.E. McGuire agreed to take over as director of the school in 1950.

Finally, Somerville's long efforts at establishing a grassroots movement appeared to be taking off. More than 200 people came out for the first meeting, representing 25 parishes and two dozen unions. The program consisted of three courses: Public Speaking and Parliamentary Procedure; The Aims and Methods of Labour Unions; and Catholic Social Doctrine, which was taught by Somerville himself. There was also a special school for managers.

At the beginning of the 1950s, Somerville was 61. His children were becoming young adults; the two boys had entered St. Augustine's Seminary on their way to the priesthood. The girls were in high school. At home, Somerville challenged the children to continually question society's assumptions. These were the years of McCarthyism in the United States, a time of fearful witch hunts for Communists sparked by Senator Joe McCarthy's hearings in the U.S. Senate. Though he was tough on Communists all his life, Somerville was no McCarthyite. Daughter Janet remembers her father challenging society's assumptions at the dinner table:

> When we would quote things that some teacher had said at school and took it for granted that we would all be fervently anti-Communist and suspect socialism, he used to help us to debate with that in our own minds and get us to withdraw from that knee-jerk thinking…. He certainly liked it when we would think. He really enjoyed that. It wasn't at all a repressed Catholic home where you couldn't criticize the clergy and you couldn't say anything disrespectful. It was a committed but critical atmosphere.

His challenge of conventional thinking did not extend to social norms or Church doctrine, however. Though sympathetic to the civil rights movement in the United States, he would have found the subsequent growth of feminism incomprehensible, his daughters believe.

Although he was not an old man, disturbing signs of Somerville's mortality appeared in the fall of 1952. A chain-smoker for many years, he began to experience health problems. In December, he received the diagnosis: cancer. The doctor said he had just a few weeks to live.

The Last Fateful Passage

Henry Somerville was a patient in St. Michael's Hospital when he received the terrible news on December 8, 1952, the feast of the Immaculate Conception. Typically, he decided that he would control the terms of his death, and even the way he was remembered. He insisted immediately that if he was going to die, he would do so at home. The family rented a hospital bed and installed it in his second-floor study. A stream of visitors came to call on him, including Cardinal McGuigan. Daughter Moira, who was 17 at the time, recalls the scene vividly; she had responded to a ring at the doorbell on a Sunday.

> There was Cardinal McGuigan and he was in full cardinal regalia, the bright red, shimmering sort of taffeta-like silk, and he had the long cape that he wore and it trailed on the ground behind him. And he wore the little biretta on his head. He had a priest with him who hung back. He said, "I have come to see your father." I think there was probably just my sisters at home and my mother. I let him in and the cardinal started to go upstairs; his long, flowing red cape filled the staircase so I couldn't get around him. I feared he wouldn't know which way to go. At the top of the stairs he looked at me and I pointed to the right and he went into the room. He said to my father, "Well, Henry, you're going to God." "Yes, your eminence." "Remember me when you get there." I fled to get Mum so I didn't hear the rest of the conversation.

Another visitor was Henry's brother Charles, a Jesuit priest in England. He came to stay for a month but had to leave before Henry died. Charles helped to settle things; one of his most important tasks was writing an obituary of his brother for *The Canadian Register*. Henry insisted on dictating it to Charles to make sure Charles got it right! Daughter Janet remembers coming home from school one day, running upstairs to see her father and stopping outside his door when she heard voices inside the room. "He was dictating his obituary syllable by syllable, and that's what appeared in *The Register*, signed by Charles Somerville."

Somerville died on February 20, 1953. "They say he died serenely and in command of his fate," recalls Janet, who was 14 at the time. The funeral was at Our Lady of Lourdes, with Cardinal McGuigan presiding and numerous priests present. He was buried at Toronto's Mount Hope Cemetery, where he was joined by his wife, Margaret, more than three decades later.

Henry Somerville left a remarkable legacy, not the least of which were five highly intelligent and talented children who, as adults, were committed to the Catholic Church. Three were to have a significant impact on the Church in Canada in the late twentieth century. Father Peter was rector of St. Augustine's Seminary, where he served for three years before his untimely death as a result of an accident in 1987. Father Stephen earned a widespread reputation as a composer of liturgical music. Janet pursued a lay career that in many ways closely paralleled her father's. She was part of a co-operative that in the late 1970s founded *Catholic New Times*, an independent Catholic weekly newspaper based in Toronto that was devoted to social justice and reform within the Church. She worked as an editor for some 20 years before being appointed the first Catholic general secretary of the Canadian Council of Churches, a post from which she retired in 2002.

Assessing the impact of Somerville's work on the larger Church is a little more difficult. He was one of a minority of intellectuals working for the Catholic Church who strove to educate the faithful about Catholic social doctrine, a part of the Church's teaching that to this day is sometimes referred to as the Church's best-kept secret. At a time when lay Catholics rarely held positions of leadership within the Church, he stood out. Historian Jeanne Beck, whose doctoral thesis on Somerville's work remains the most in-depth scholarly study on the subject, includes him in a long list of illustrious Catholics of like mind: Father Charles Plater, Francis Cardinal Bourne (Archbishop of Westminster), G.K. Chesterton and Hilaire Belloc in the United Kingdom; Father John Ryan and Dorothy Day in the United States; Toronto Archbishop Neil McNeil, Father James Tompkins, Father Moses Coady and Catherine de Hueck Doherty in Canada. In Beck's assessment,

> Henry Somerville was, for many years, particularly during the 1930s, the most influential layman in the English-speaking Catholic Church in Canada…. He accepted the teaching of the Church and never wavered from it…. He took care that *The Register* did not become a forum for the consideration of ideas that could lead to theological controversy, though he never hesitated to take up the cudgels for other causes with which he was passionately involved. Rather, his principal concern was to arouse the Church's awareness about the shape and quality of Canadian society in the light of the papal teaching on the subject.

He had his share of successes and failures. Despite his game efforts, his study groups and adult education classes never really gained popularity, though there were flares of interest. However, his advisory role with two of Toronto's archbishops, McNeil and McGuigan – both forward-thinking men – was key to their own promotion of social doctrine. Somerville can take credit for helping the Catholic Church in Canada reconcile itself with and influence the left-wing political movements in Canada, notably within trade unions and the CCF.

Less concrete, but real nevertheless, was his influence on a younger generation of Catholic activists who would come into their own in the 1960s and 1970s after the Second Vatican Council placed new emphasis on the importance of the laity. This group would carve out a growing niche within the Church that worked to bring to life its social encyclicals and place the Church in solidarity with the poor and oppressed. They would apply a similar critique of global economics and politics to the one Somerville used, developing the "see, judge, act" method of social analysis leading to action. Somerville and his contemporaries laid the groundwork for them. Though not a theological reformer, Somerville believed the true Catholic did not simply go to church on Sunday. Their task was to challenge society wherever it strayed from the principles of human rights, dignity and respect – to be prophetic figures, laying a straight path for the Lord in the secular wilderness of the twentieth century.

Toronto is a long way from Leeds, England – 5,538 kilometres, to be exact. Henry Somerville travelled far in his lifetime, making that stormy passage across the Atlantic Ocean nine times. And 1953 was a long way from 1889. In that space of 63 years, Somerville had passed through several ages: the end of the Industrial Revolution; a goodbye to Victorian times; the terror of modern warfare in the First World War; the Roaring Twenties; the Great Depression; the Second World War; and, as we learned in the war's waning years, the awesome horror of the Holocaust, which forced us to confront the soul-destroying realization that evil is a far greater power in the world than our pretensions of modern sophistication will allow. He had a close look at the beginning of the Cold War and no doubt found cold comfort in seeing his lifelong suspicions of Communism confirmed. Yet, from his editor's desk in Toronto, he looked out on the world and, despite the evil he saw, still found God's creation to be good – and worth fighting for.

From that Leeds ghetto, Somerville had also risen far. A more likely fate for a son of an unskilled labourer would have been to follow in his father's footsteps, even working in the same factory, as the young Henry had done at age 13. But his innate talent and drive would not allow him to stay there. Perhaps we could say that God wouldn't either – or at least one of his servants, Father Charles Plater, S.J., who noticed the fervent young Catholic firebrand and decided to direct his intelligence and energy towards more fruitful endeavours, wouldn't. From there, Somerville's path zigged and zagged over England and Europe, back and forth between Canada and Great Britain. A quick glance at his life's path would suggest a gadfly or opportunist, jumping constantly to the next new thing. But Somerville was not that way; he was seriously devoted both to his chosen craft of journalism and to his faith. Despite all the passages to and fro over the decades, his pursuit of each of these kept his path straight.

From his early years as a sub-editor at the *Manchester Guardian* to his dying days as he dictated his own obituary, Somerville remained a writer, advocate, teacher, analyst, critic, reporter – in sum, a journalist. Yet his efforts were clearly not made for the usual lures of journalism: glamour, fame and fortune, being at the centre of history in the making. These were in short supply for the editor of a small weekly religious newspaper. He could have had a more traditional trajectory to his journalistic career: a starting point at the famed *Guardian* was already a leap ahead of the majority of rookies in the field. A far more comfortable and illustrious life was there, if he had just stayed put. But something more drove him, something that drives many journalists (if you dig beneath their surface cynicism) but is slowly buried by years of chronicling humanity's dark side. In Somerville, this something burned hot throughout his life.

Somerville did not just believe in God and practise the usual sacramental devotions that went with his lifelong adherence to the Roman Catholic Church. He believed that God had asked him to do a little work for him, to use the talents he had for researching, writing and speaking to help make the world a better place. He believed the Church's pontiffs had been divinely inspired, giving him the theological tools he needed to see and explain the world, and that these could work in partnership with modern economic and political philosophy, which emphasized individual freedom and human rights. He believed the Church's mission was as important for the modern world as it had been in the first century. As the early Church had adapted and accepted the best of its surrounding culture, he thought that modernity (despite the existence of so much evil) had much the Church could use. Mostly, he firmly believed that God intended the world's lowly – the kind of poor, undereducated, unhealthy, forgotten people he grew up with – to have a better life on earth. There was nothing preordained about the existing order of things; nothing said the rules of capitalism were created by God and could not be disobeyed. He was convinced that God did not intend the rich to oppress the poor or the poor to remain forever the victims of a harsh, cruel world. The task that fell to the journalist from Leeds was to show that those he felt most kinship with could, with a little education, do exactly what he did.

It was because of his tenacity in following this path that he left a distinctive mark on the world. Many men and women in the twentieth century were full of idealism and new, fashionable ideas. They all wanted to change the world. But, for so many of them, God was just another idea to be discarded with the old-fashioned notions of the nineteenth century. Somerville knew God was not an idea, but a real, all-loving being who could no more be rationalized out of existence than could the evil in the world that Somerville fought so ardently. God had called him and he had said, "Here I am, Lord."

Henry Somerville tried to live this conviction at home, with his family, at work in his dealings with others, and in the words he put to paper. As is often the case, success was hard to measure. But that didn't really matter, because he kept his eyes set on the long road, on the ultimate journey, caring little about the obstacles, working as hard as he could until he could work no longer, remaining faithful until the end.

Bibliography

Books and Articles

Alexander, Anne. *The Antigonish Movement: Moses Coady and Adult Education Today.* Toronto: Thompson Educational Publishing, 1997.

Baum, Gregory. *Catholics and Canadian Socialism.* Toronto: James Lorimer, 1980.

Beck, Jeanne R. *Henry Somerville and the Development of Catholic Social Thought in Canada: Somerville's Role in the Archdiocese of Toronto, 1915–1943.* Ph.D. dissertation, McMaster University, 1977.

Bédarida, François. *A Social History of England, 1851–1975.* Translated by A.S. Forster. London: Methuen, 1979.

Boorstin, Daniel J. *The Seekers: The Story of Man's Continuing Quest to Understand His World.* Toronto: Random House, 1998.

Boyle, George. *Pioneer in Purple: The Life and Work of Archbishop Neil McNeil.* Montreal: Palm Publishers, 1951.

Brown, Craig, ed. *The Illustrated History of Canada.* Toronto: Lester & Orpen Dennys, 1987.

Cranston, J.H. *Ink on My Fingers.* Toronto: Ryerson Press, 1953.

Fay, Terence J. *A History of Canadian Catholics: Gallicanism, Romanism and Canadianism.* Montreal: McGill-Queen's University Press, 2002.

Daly, Bernard M. *Remembering for Tomorrow: A History of the Canadian Conference of Catholic Bishops, 1943–1993.* Ottawa: Canadian Conference of Catholic Bishops, 1995.

Gilbert, Martin. *The First World War: A Complete History.* New York: Henry Holt, 1994.

Granatstein, J.L. and Desmond Morton. *A Nation Forged in Fire: Canadians and the Second World War, 1939–1945.* Toronto: Lester & Orpen Dennys, 1989.

Hobsbawm, Eric. *Age of Extremes: The Short Twentieth Century, 1914–1991.* London: Abacus, 1995.

James, Lawrence. *The Rise and Fall of the British Empire.* New York: St. Martin's Press, 1994.

McGowan, Mark George. *The Waning of the Green: Catholics, the Irish, and Identity in Toronto, 1887–1922.* Montreal: McGill-Queen's University Press, 1999.

McGowan, Mark George and Brian P. Clarke, eds. *Catholics at the "Gathering Place": Historical Essays on the Archdiocese of Toronto 1841–1991*. Toronto: The Canadian Catholic Historical Association, 1993.

McGuigan, Peter. "Robert Keyserlingk, Cardinal McGuigan and the demise of *The Ensign*." Academic paper to be published by *Catholic Insight* in 2003.

Pearce, Joseph. *Old Thunder: A Life of Hilaire Belloc*. Fort Collins, CO: Ignatius Press, 2002.

Saywell, John T. *'Just Call Me Mitch': The Life of Mitchell F. Hepburn*. Toronto: University of Toronto Press, 1991.

Stacey, C.P. *Canada and the Age of Conflict, Vol. 2, 1921–1948*. Toronto: University of Toronto Press, 1981.

Thompson, E.P. *The Making of the English Working Class*. Harmondsworth, Middlesex, England: Penguin Books, 1984.

Webb, R.K. *Modern England* (Second Edition). New York: Harper and Row, 1980.

Papal Encyclicals

Leo XIII. *Rerum Novarum* (On the Condition of the Working Classes). Authorized English translation by Pauline Books and Media, 2000.

Pius XI. *Quadragesimo Anno* (On Social Reconstruction). Authorized English translation by Pauline Books and Media, 2000.

Pius XI. *Mit Brennender Sorge* (On the Church and the German Reich). Authorized English translation from Vatican web site www.vatican.va.

Writings by Henry Somerville

The Catholic Register, hundreds of assorted columns, editorials and articles, 1915–1918, 1933–1953.

Rome and Home. Toronto: The Canadian Register, 1947.

Studies in the Catholic Social Movement. London: Burns, Oates & Washbourne, 1933.

Other Primary Documents

Letters and dispatches to Archbishop Neil McNeil by Henry Somerville. Papers of Archbishop Neil McNeil, Archives of the Archdiocese of Toronto.

Letters to James Cardinal McGuigan, Archbishop of Toronto, by Henry Somerville. Papers of James Cardinal McGuigan, Archives of the Archdiocese of Toronto.

Letters by Henry Somerville and Peter Somerville, from the private collection of Father Stephen Somerville.

Interviews with the Author

Janet Somerville
Moira Van Nooten (née Somerville)
Father Stephen Somerville
Alfred de Manche
Monsignor Thomas Raby
Father Joseph O'Neill

Gem: The Life of Sister Mac
Sister Geraldine MacNamara

Eleanor Stebner
Foreword by Rosemary Radford Ruether

GEM is a "social-spiritual" biography that explores how Sister Geraldine MacNamara – a privileged, middle-class, well-educated religious sister – lived into her vocation and became converted to social justice.

A member of the Sisters of the Holy Names of Jesus and Mary, MacNamara in 1976 founded Rossbrook House, a drop-in centre in one of Winnipeg's more troubled neighbourhoods. From Rossbrook, MacNamara and her "kids" addressed issues crucial to their community – including social services, substance abuse, truancy, the justice system and urban development. MacNamara herself became a well-known local and national advocate for the rights of the disenfranchised, especially the young urban poor.

MacNamara was influenced by her personal experiences, idealism and sense of commitment; by the vision of Vatican II and its uplifting of the people of God; and especially by the young people she met, the friendships she made, and the struggles she witnessed.

A Faith that Challenges
The Life of Jim McSheffrey

Maura Hanrahan
Foreword by Helen Fogwill Porter

A Faith that Challenges tells the story of Jim McSheffrey, a Jesuit brother who shared all he had with those around him. For Jim, a commitment to the Gospel values of justice and peace meant living in a low-income neighbourhood – sharing the burdens of people living in poverty, learning from their struggles, celebrating their spirit, and opening his home and heart to them. He marched on Confederation Building when the Newfoundland government instituted a fee for children who took the bus to school. He co-founded a community garden so his neighbours could have fresh vegetables and develop a relationship with each other and with the land. He greatly valued his friends and proudly presented them with garage-sale bargains or items he found in people's curbside trash, sure that the broken-down lawnmower or propane stove he had picked up would come in handy. He refused to attend fancy dinners at expensive hotels. He brought many people together, and was often a thorn in the side of those in authority.

Other Novalis Biographies

The Doctor Will Not See You Now
The Autobiography of a Blind Physician

Jane Poulson

Jane Poulson was dealt a difficult hand of cards as a child: diabetes. Blinded by this disease at 27 and about to graduate from medical school, Jane pushed herself to become Canada's first practising blind physician. Then, when cancer and heart disease took their toll on her, she continued to live the only way she knew how – with every ounce of strength and courage and hope she possessed. She embraced life as a uniquely gifted doctor with a special understanding of disease that only her degree of affliction and hard-earned faith could teach. In recognition of her exceptional medical skills and insight, she was awarded the Order of Canada at the age of 35. Although her life was cut short, she lived it to the fullest and leaves her readers with a joyous account of her triumph over incredible odds.

Other Novalis Biographies

Faith and Freedom
The Life and Times of Bill Ryan SJ

Bob Chodos and Jamie Swift

Bill Ryan's life story is a lens through which we can view the tensions and accomplishments of the past 50 turbulent years of Church history. From humble origins in the Ottawa Valley, Ryan went to Harvard and eventually became leader of the Canadian Jesuits and General Secretary of the Canadian Conference of Catholic Bishops. He has been an agent of both social and religious change in Canada and beyond. During the aftermath of the Vietnam war, his base was the Center for Concern, the Washington-based think tank. Through extensive travel and consultation, Ryan shares his insights into community and development on a global scale, and continues to explore issues of faith, economics, social justice and globalization.

NOVALIS

**To order these and other
fine books, contact Novalis**

**1-877-702-7773
or
cservice@novalis.ca**